A WILLIAMSON ❤ KIDS CAN! BOOK

THE KiDS' MULTiCULTURAL ART BOOK

ART BOOK

Art & Craft Experiences from Around the World

ALEXANDRA M. TERZIAN

WILLIAMSON PUBLISHING • CHARLOTTE, VERMONT 05445

CONTENTS

• Acknowledgements •

I am grateful to my family for supporting me during the labor of this book. I am very grateful to my daughter, Annie, for her ideas and contributions from a child's perspective.

I would like to thank Sherrie Dorr and Wendy Wilson who taught an inservice course on cultural diversity for Montgomery County Public Schools that changed my life.

I would like to thank the librarians and assistants at Montgomery Blair High School, especially Erica K. Lodish and R.B. Lasco. Thank you for letting me check out books indefinitely without consequences.

Thank you also to my friend and colleague Diane Swift for her contributions in the African chapter.

Thank you to my former student teacher, Kathie Grove, who turned me on to the beauty of the Northwest Coast Indians.

I am also grateful to all my colleagues in the Montgomery County Public Schools who helped me with ideas and gave me their support during the making of this book.

I thank Susan Williamson and Jennifer Ingersoll of Williamson Publishing Company for their editorial skills in the revision of the text.

I thank Dr. Ann Richardson, Aesthetic Education Department, Montgomery County Public Schools, for her moral support when I needed it and her dedication to multiculturalism.

Most of all I would like to thank all the students who have helped me with ideas, shared their cultural heritage with me, and who supported my efforts to bring multicultural art into the classroom.

A LETTER FROM MRS. T

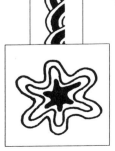

Dear Fellow Artist and Reader,

Welcome to the world of multicultural art! I believe the best way to understand and appreciate another culture is by meeting its people, eating its food, listening to its music, and by creating its arts and crafts. The arts and crafts in this book were inspired by many different cultures and traditions around the world and in the United States and Canada.

I have collected artifacts (man-made objects) from many distant lands, and I have been fortunate enough to visit museums the world over and see authentic art and artifacts created by people hundreds of years ago, as well as today. Maybe some day you will travel to other countries of the world and around the United States and Canada. When you do, you can visit museums, and also start your own collection of artifacts. Actually, if you visit a museum in any big city near your home, you will likely see some wonderful multicultural art. Meanwhile, I hope you enjoy making these artifacts and becoming familiar with some of the world's rich cultural traditions.

I have been an artist and a teacher for many years. I have learned many things from my students, my children, my friends, and from other teachers. I am pleased to share these ideas with you in this book. Please write to me and let me know how your multicultural art projects turn out, and share some of your ideas and ethnic traditions with me. I will value your thoughts and ideas.

Sincerely,

Alexandra M. Terzian

Mrs. T.

To write to Mrs. T, send your letter to Mrs. A.M. Terzian, c/o Williamson Publishing Co., P.O.Box 185, Charlotte, Vermont 05445, USA

GETTING STARTED

If you are already wondering which craft to try first, then I know you are going to have a wonderful time "visiting" other cultures with this book. There are so many things to choose from no matter what your interests — making useful artifacts, decorative crafts, ceremonial art, or wonderful ethnic gifts. Feel free to begin anywhere right away. Very likely you'll have everything you need in your home, since most of the crafts use paper, glue, markers, and odds and ends found in most homes.

When you are waiting for something to dry before proceeding on a project, however, it would be a good idea to read this introductory section (or have an older person read it to you), because I have collected some art tips here, rather than repeating them over and over throughout the book. So take a few moments to familiarize yourself with some of these hints, so you can go forward with great creative confidence!

CREATIVITY COUNTS!

Just as each culture brings its own richness to our world, so, too, are the projects' richness and beauty made whole by your personal, creative style. Every person will visualize a project

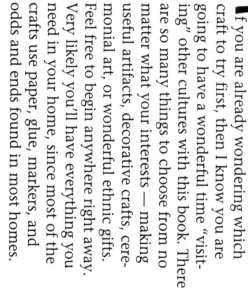

differently — that's what makes you special and unique. Cut and paste, or color and paint, however YOU wish. There is no right or wrong way to create and craft shapes and designs. In some projects there are suggestions for colors or shapes, but these are only for your general guidance. You should feel free to do something completely different. In fact, I hope that you do many things in ways I haven't even thought of yet! If you don't have something on a project's materials list, be creative and investigate a substitute. With the exception of salt dough or papier-mache recipes, there are no right ways to do anything; using different materials can result in a richer, more enlightening experience. So, please, set your inhibitions aside and have fun!

CAN I DO IT?

If you are wondering if certain projects are too difficult for you, let me assure you that most every project in the book can be done — one way or another — by everyone. Some projects are very simple to do, but you may want to take a lot of time perfecting the design you paint on it. Others may be more challenging to assemble, but once that is done, it will be easy to cover with papier-mache and to paint. Certainly, there are some projects in here where you may need to ask for a little help from an older person, and that is ex-

actly what you should do. Other times you may decide to change the way a project is done because it makes more sense to you another way, and that is fine, too. I have purposely not rated these crafts with degree of difficulty because I believe that in your own way and perhaps with some help, you can create something quite wonderful. The secret to success is simply to express your own creativity.

FOR SAFETY'S SAKE!

Whenever you are using art and craft tools and supplies, you need to be careful. Think about your safety and the safety of those around you. Be especially careful if there is a baby around you. Keep all of your tools and supplies away from the edge of the table. Here are some other safety tips:

• All supplies, materials, and ingredients in this book are nontoxic. As a rule, when working with art supplies, it is a good idea to have good ventilation around you.

• If you are supposed to use *safety scissors*, then please use them. Older helpers can cut the parts that need pointed scissors for you.

• In a few projects, you will need to use a *mat knife*, or a *craft knife*. Please have an older helper use this very sharp tool. Remind your older helper to cut on

some thick cardboard so as not to damage your table.

• *Balloons* are fun, but they can be very dangerous for young children, causing choking if they put the balloons in their mouths. Never put balloon parts in your mouth. Keep all balloons, balloon parts, or uninflated balloons out of any child's reach. If a balloon pops, be sure to pick up all the pieces.

• Although it is good to recycle styrofoam products, do not reuse *styrofoam meat trays* that have had meat on them. Even after washing, these trays may be contaminated from the meat residue. Instead, cut a paper plate in the tray's shape, and proceed with your project.

• ART SUPPLIES AND RECYCLING •

There are very few supplies that need to be bought to create the wonderful artifacts in this book. For the most part, you can scrounge around your home, and come up with everything you need and then some.

- **Basic Supplies**

  Construction paper, mixed colors

  Poster board, several sheets, some white

  Glue

  Markers, black and other colors

  Tempera paints, dark and light colors

  Acrylic gloss varnish (available at most art stores)

  White paper plates, inexpensive, 7", 8", or 9"

  Wooden tongue depressors or Popsicle sticks

- **Basic Tools**

  Small stapler or regular stapler

  Scissors

  Hole punch

  Mat knife, or craft knife

  Paintbrushes

- **Recycled Collectibles**

  Scrap white paper such as typing paper and computer paper (use blank side for making patterns)

  Paper cups, small and large

  Toilet tissue tubes and paper towel tubes

  Paper pulp egg cartons

  Styrofoam peanuts used for stuffing

  Cardboard backing and boxes

  Aluminum foil, wiped clean and dried

  Plastic margarine containers

  Used gift wrap

  Scrap yarn and string

  Scrap poster board

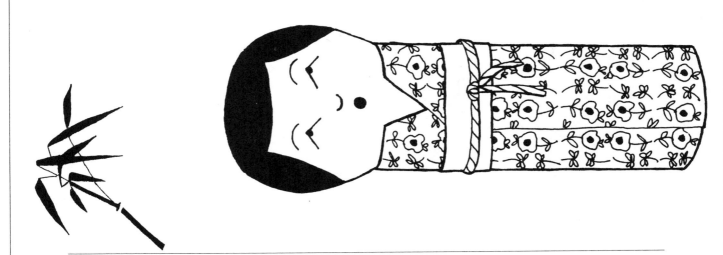

HELPFUL HINTS

• Cover your work area with newspaper (and the floor around your work area). That way you can be as carefree as you like, without worrying about making a mess that will be hard to clean up.

• Want to really surprise a grown-up? Here are two ways: Always wear an old art shirt or smock. (You can decorate it or just wait and let various spills and splashes decorate it.) Also, try this trick: When mixing tempera paint, add a small amount of dish-washing liquid to it. This not only aids washing out paint stains, it also prevents paint from chipping off the projects when they are dry.

• Tempera paint can be improved with a little acrylic gloss varnish (available at any art store). This prevents paint chipping and will leave your crafts with a shiny finish.

• Be sure to wash all paintbrushes with water. Keep a jar of water handy so you can wash your brushes out as you go along.

• Recycle styrofoam egg cartons into paint palettes. Each section of an egg carton will hold a different color and will stay fresh if you close the lid tightly with a piece of tape.

• Tell your family you are starting a Re-cycle Art Box. Post a list of what you are trying to reuse and recycle on the refrigerator, and ask them to help you. Decorate and label the box and keep it in a closet or in your room.

• An inexpensive, handy way to organize your smaller art supplies is in a fishing tackle box. The small top sections are ideal for storing paper clips, erasers, buttons, sequins, and chalk. The bottom section can hold markers, brushes, sponges, pencils, folded paper towels, fabric scraps, and other great art finds.

AND NOW HAVE FUN...

These tips and hints are just some things I learned from my experiences that I thought you would find helpful. There are no rules for doing anything — just have a wonderful time discovering all the interesting things about the creativity of the cultures in the world around us. At the same time, discover all the wonderful creativity that is already inside of you.

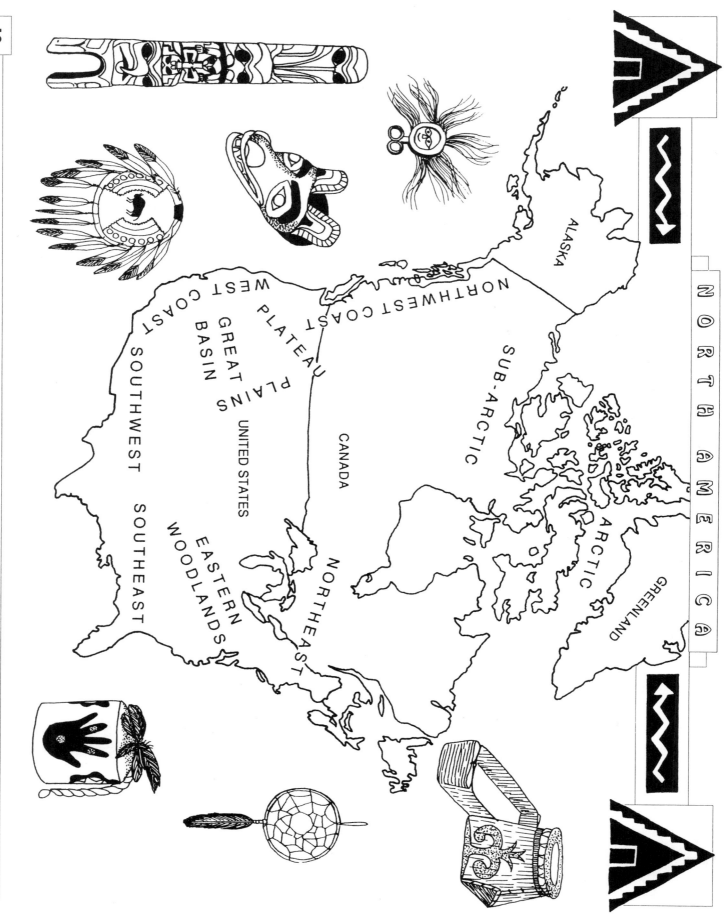

NORTH AMERICA

ALASKA

NORTHWEST COAST

WEST COAST

PLATEAU

GREAT BASIN

PLAINS

SUB-ARCTIC

ARCTIC

GREENLAND

SOUTHWEST

UNITED STATES

CANADA

SOUTHEAST

EASTERN WOODLANDS

NORTHEAST

NATIVE AMERICANS of NORTH AMERICA

Imagine, if you could walk from Asia to North America, just how long it would take! Well, that's just what the first Native Americans did when they migrated, or moved, to the countries we now call North, Central, and South America. You see, these regions weren't always surrounded by water. That's right, the continent of North America

once was connected to Asia by a great glacier bridge that extended across the ocean — about 10,000 to 40,000 years ago! When the glaciers that provided the bridge melted, the sea rose, and the bridge was gone. This made it impossible for people or animals to get across the ocean without a boat.

So by the time Christopher Columbus sailed from Europe to the New World in 1492, these people — whom we now call Native American Indians — had already been making this "new" land their home for thousands of years!

Today, using the rich and ancient traditions of their ancestors, many Native American Indians and Eskimos keep the heritage from long ago alive through their beautiful arts, crafts, and traditions. In many parts of the United

States, you can buy handmade jewelry, rugs, or wood carvings made by different tribal groups or nations of Native Americans. But what better way to appreciate and better understand this rich culture than by creating your own Indian-style crafts inspired by these wonderfully creative people!

Begin your special journey by diving into these arts and crafts with a box of crayons, paper, and a whole bunch of imagination. You'll learn why buffalo were so important to the Plains Indians, for example, when you make a *Sun Dance Skull*. Or, learn how the Chippewa warded off bad dreams by making your own *Dream Catcher* to hang above your pillow.

Since there were so many different groups of Native Americans, it seems

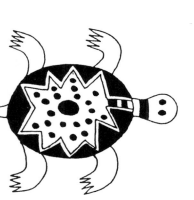

only natural that a wide variety of artistic designs and decorative symbols came into being. But where did Native Americans get their inspiration to create such beautiful arts and crafts? The natural world around them — the sea, fish, trees, birds, and other wildlife — played an important role and created a passion in their hearts that's seen in many of their fine art creations. For example, the Flathead of the Plateau (pla-TOE) continue to make vests with the loveliest flower designs. The Lakota-Sioux (soo) of the Plains use diamond and triangular shapes. Each tribal group also makes pottery designs and patterns that distinguish them from other groups.

Native Americans have long had a strong relationship with Mother Earth and want to preserve the environment for the many generations of children to come. Making a *Storyteller Animal Mask* will help you understand how the Northwest Coast Indians taught their children important lessons about life.

Mask-making is a traditional Eskimo, or Inuit, craft you will learn about, too. Make your own *Eskimo Laughing Mask* and gather a group of friends to partake in a fun game that's been enjoyed by Eskimos for many years. One thing is for sure, you're certain to have hours of fun making these Native American crafts, while learning about the cultures that give them their splendor.

BROWN BAG VEST

Made from a simple brown paper bag, you can decorate your own Native American vest with authentic Indian designs or your own colorful creations.

◆ **M A T E R I A L S** ◆

Plain brown paper grocery bag

Tempera paint or markers, any colors you wish

Yarn, 2 pieces about 12" long

Scissors, hole punch

1. Cut up the middle of the front of the bag and around the neck area as shown. Cut into the sides and make two armholes.

2. Cut fringe all the way around the bottom.

3. To make the ties, punch two holes near the neck opening at the front. Pass a piece of yarn through each hole, and knot each piece at both ends.

4. Decorate with markers or tempera paints, using the illustrated Native American designs, if you wish.

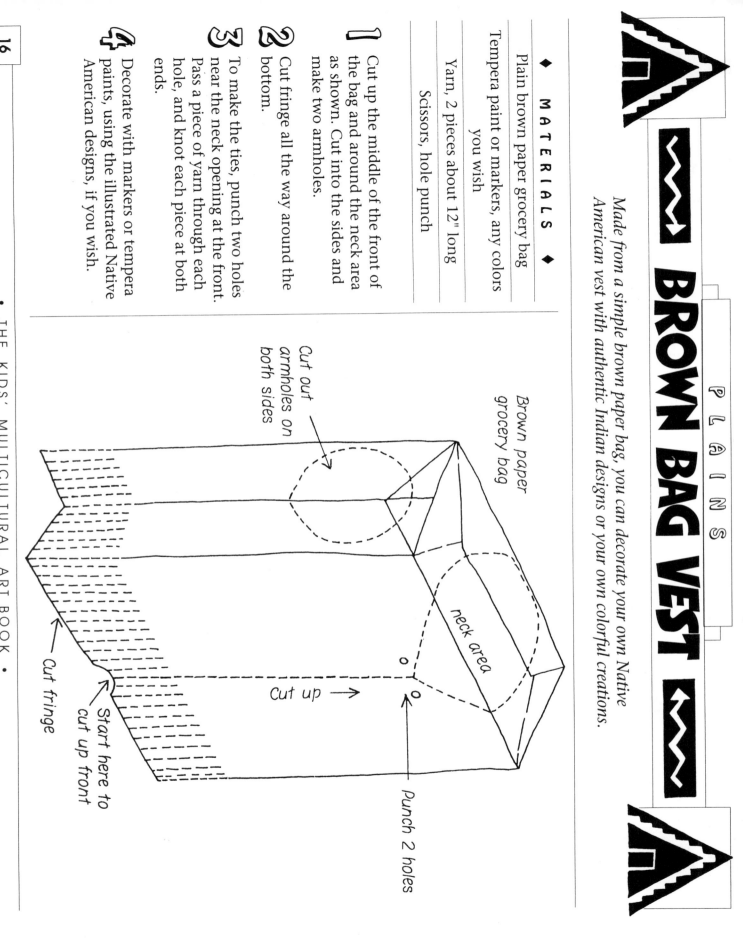

Brown paper grocery bag

Cut out armholes on both sides

neck area

Cut up →

Punch 2 holes

Start here to cut up front

Cut fringe

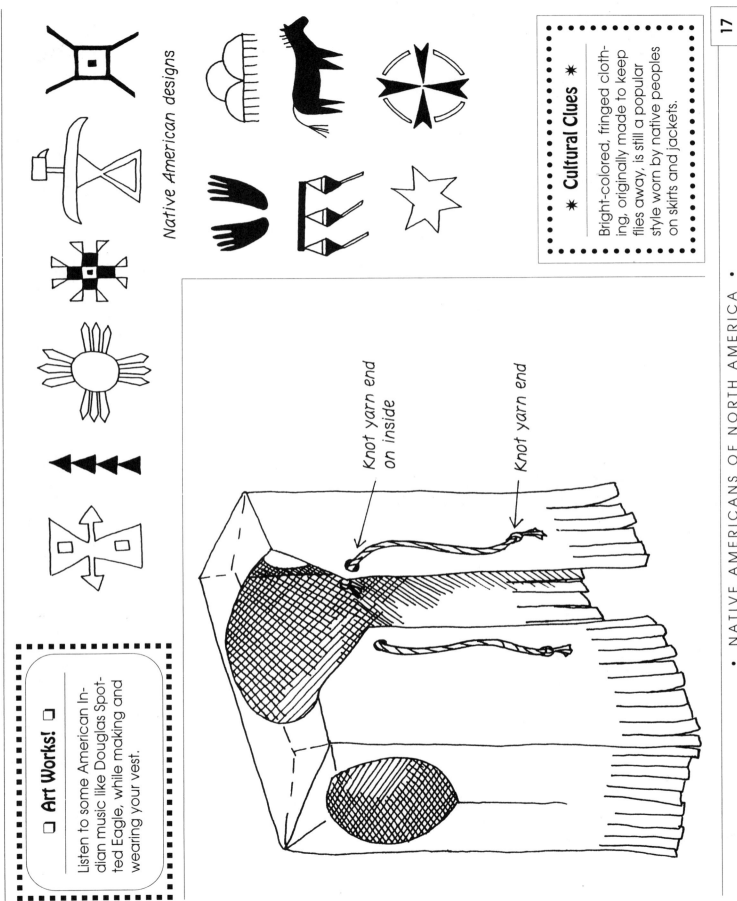

Native American designs

❋ Cultural Clues ❋

Bright-colored, fringed clothing, originally made to keep flies away, is still a popular style worn by native peoples on skirts and jackets.

☐ Art Works! ☐

Listen to some American Indian music like Douglas Spotted Eagle, while making and wearing your vest.

Knot yarn end on inside

Knot yarn end

MAGIC POWER SHIELD

Plains Indians made rawhide shields decorated with pictures of spirits they believed would protect them during battles. They also used a "medicine" bag or bundle (that carried magic charms) when they went into battle.

◆ MATERIALS ◆

Poster board circle, 6" or 7"

Yarn or string, 2 pieces, 16" and 8" long

Beads, 3 or 4, and feather

Markers, hole punch

1. Punch holes around the paper circle's edge about 1" apart.

2. Use markers to decorate the paper shield with Native American designs.

3. Tape one end of the yarn, and poke it into the top hole and pull through. Leave about 3" at the end for the loop later.

4. Go in and out of the holes, bringing the taped end of the yarn back to the top hole. Tie this to the other end.

5. Cut a piece of yarn about 8" long. Loop it through the bottom hole and even the ends.

6. Pass 3 or 4 beads up the yarn and slip a feather into the beads as shown. Knot both ends of the yarn to keep the feather secure.

7. Add more feathers around the circle the same way. Hang on the wall.

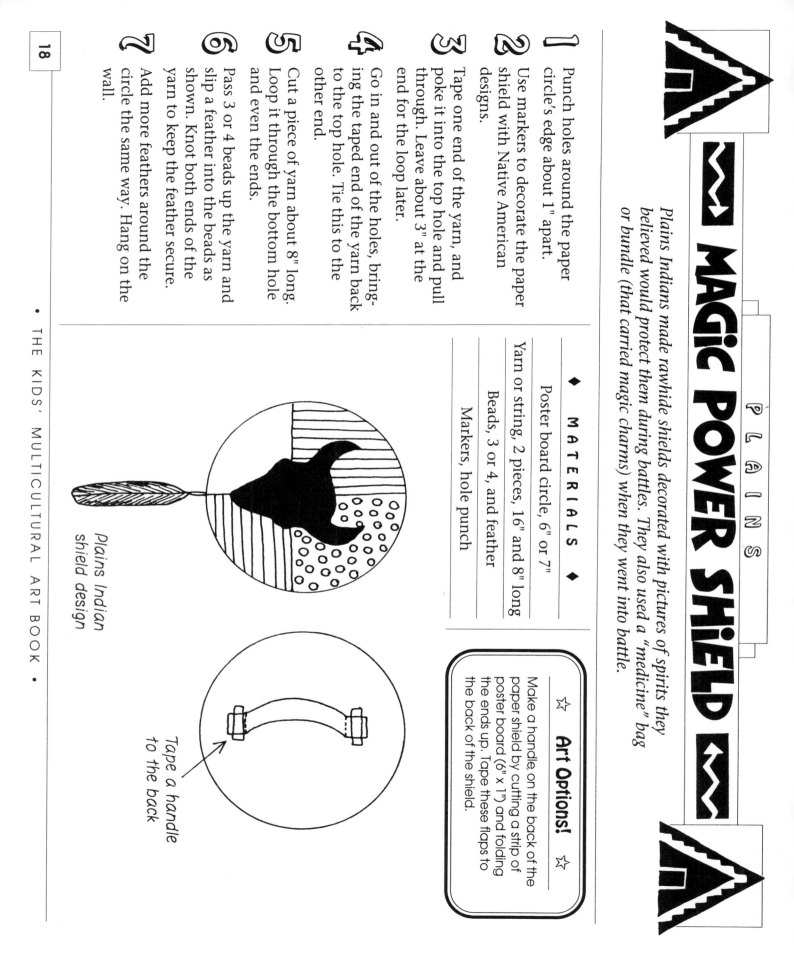

Plains Indian shield design

☆ Art Options! ☆

Make a handle on the back of the paper shield by cutting a strip of poster board (6" x 1") and folding the ends up. Tape these flaps to the back of the shield.

Tape a handle to the back

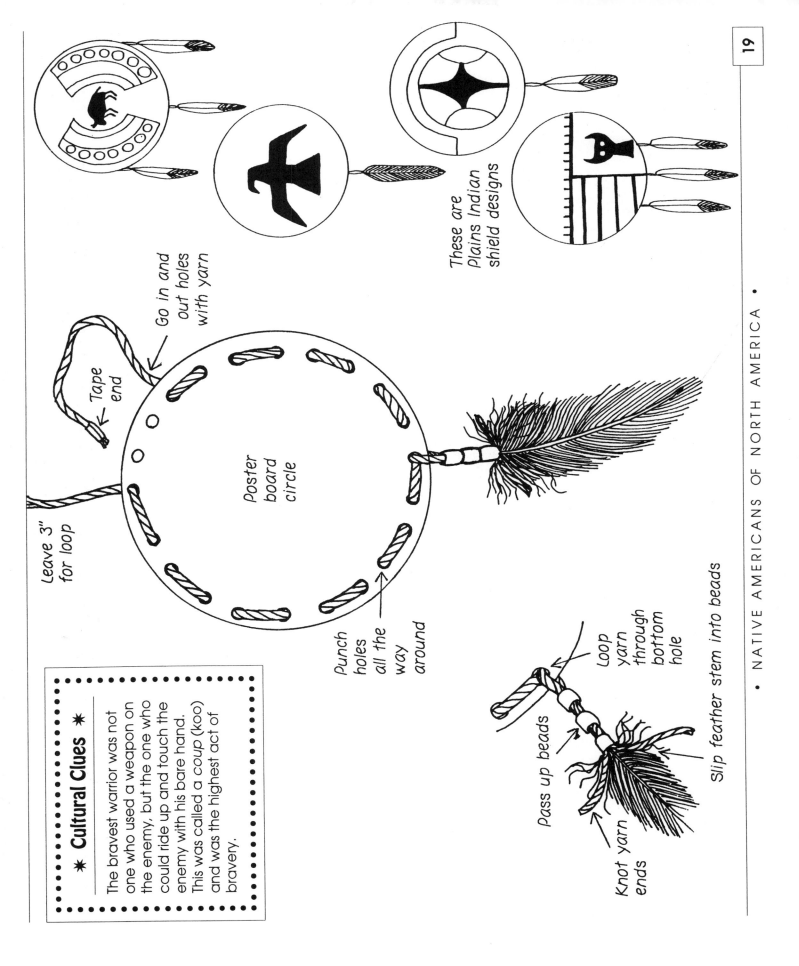

These are Plains Indian shield designs

Go in and out holes with yarn

Tape end

Leave 3" for loop

Poster board circle

Punch holes all the way around

Loop yarn through bottom hole

Pass up beads

Slip feather stem into beads

Knot yarn ends

☀ Cultural Clues ☀

The bravest warrior was not one who used a weapon on the enemy, but the one who could ride up and touch the enemy with his bare hand. This was called a coup (koo) and was the highest act of bravery.

PLAINS

LAKOTA-SIOUX CHARM BAG

Indians hunted animals like buffalo, moose, deer, and rabbits for food and for their skins. Small pieces of skin were softened to be used for pouches and bags. A medicine man, or healer, might have charms, shells, and special herbs in a charm bag to help someone who was sick.

◆ **M A T E R I A L S** ◆

Felt, any light color, 9" x 11"

Scrap paper, about 8¹/₂" x 11"

Yarn, to hang bag around your neck

Pencil, stapler, hole punch, scissors

Beads, needle and thread for decoration

1 Trace the bag pattern onto the scrap paper and cut out.

2 Fold the felt in half the short way. Lay the paper pattern so that the flat edge (see dotted line in illustration) is on the fold of the felt. Trace the pattern onto the felt.

3 Keep the felt folded and cut around the tracing, but don't cut on the folded edge.

4 Fold *one* rounded edge down as shown for the front opening. Staple this flap down (be careful not to staple through to the other side of the bag).

5 Keep the two sides of the felt together and staple closed.

6 Hole punch two holes at the top rounded edge of the bag. Pass the yarn through as shown, even the ends, and tie.

7 Sew or glue on beads and scraps of felt for decoration.

8 Add a lucky charm to your bag and hang around your neck.

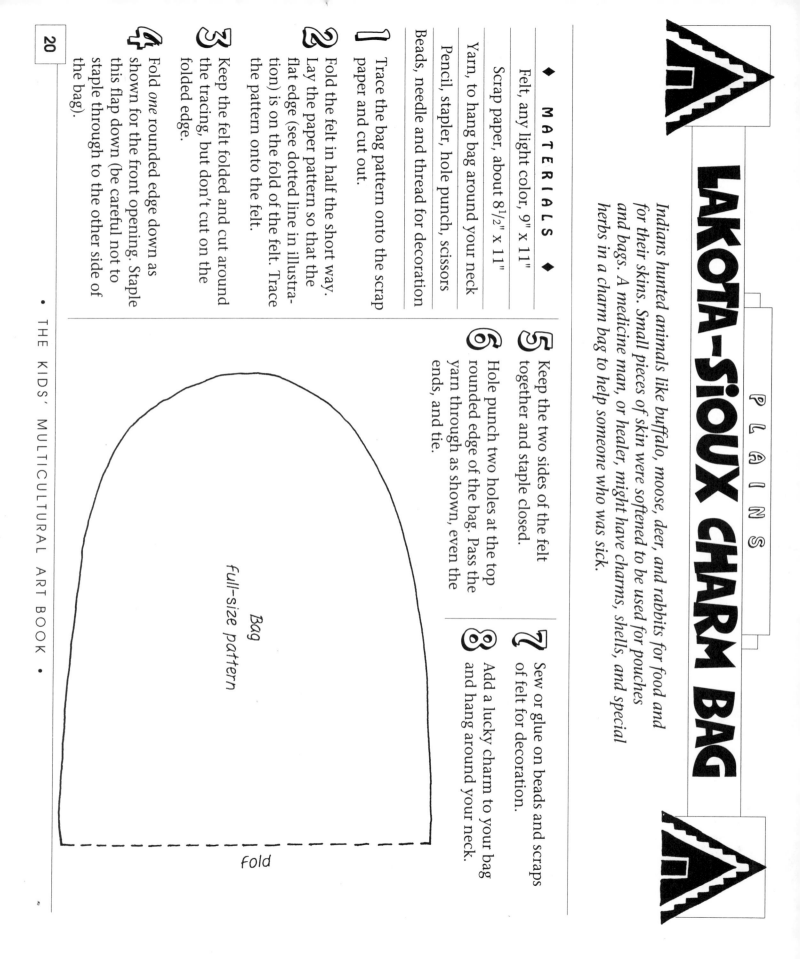

Bag
full-size pattern

Fold

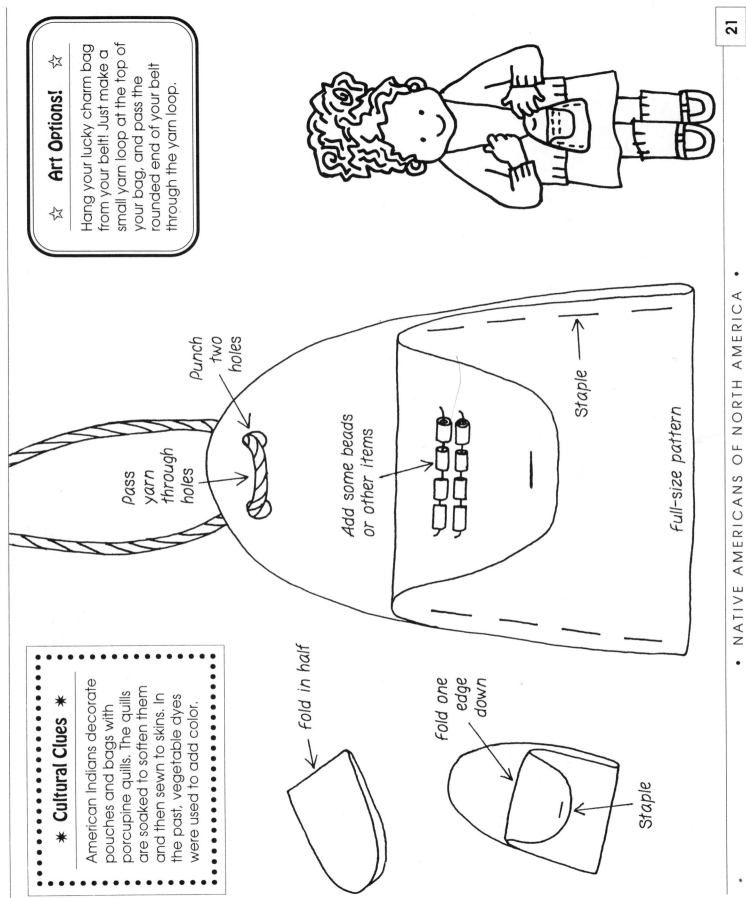

☆ **Art Options!** ☆

Hang your lucky charm bag from your belt! Just make a small yarn loop at the top of your bag, and pass the rounded end of your belt through the yarn loop.

Punch two holes

Pass yarn through holes

Add some beads or other items

Staple

Full-size pattern

✷ **Cultural Clues** ✷

American Indians decorate pouches and bags with porcupine quills. The quills are soaked to soften them and then sewn to skins. In the past, vegetable dyes were used to add color.

Fold in half

Fold one edge down

Staple

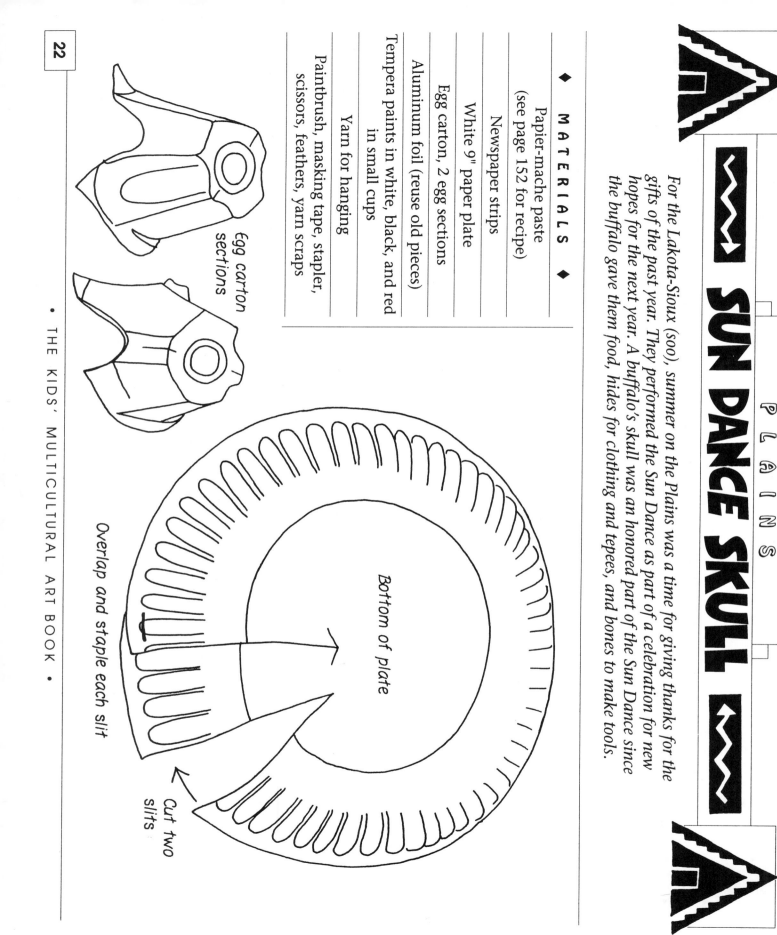

PLAINS

SUN DANCE SKULL

For the Lakota-Sioux (SOO), summer on the Plains was a time for giving thanks for the gifts of the past year. They performed the Sun Dance as part of a celebration for new hopes for the next year. A buffalo's skull was an honored part of the Sun Dance since the buffalo gave them food, hides for clothing and tepees, and bones to make tools.

◆ MATERIALS ◆

Papier-mache paste
(see page 152 for recipe)

Newspaper strips

White 9" paper plate

Egg carton, 2 egg sections

Aluminum foil (reuse old pieces)

Tempera paints in white, black, and red in small cups

Yarn for hanging

Paintbrush, masking tape, stapler, scissors, feathers, yarn scraps

egg carton sections

Bottom of plate

Overlap and staple each slit

Cut two slits

1 Cut two slits in the paper plate, and staple so that the plate bends in the middle.

2 Tape the egg carton sections on for the eye sockets.

3 To make the horns, shape two pieces of foil to about 8" long. Staple each horn to the *back* of the paper plate at the top.

4 Place crumpled up newspaper under the paper plate for support while you work. Follow directions on page 152 for applying newspaper and papier-mache paste. Cover the skull form, front and back, with one layer of newspaper strips (except for the tops of the egg carton sections). Let dry overnight.

Crumple up foil and shape into horns. Staple to back of form

Tape on egg carton sections for eyes

Wrap newspaper strips around horns, and front and back

5 Add a second layer of newspaper strips and let dry overnight.

6 Paint the skull with two coats of white tempera paint on the front and back. Let dry.

7 Paint dots and stripes with red and black paint, as shown. Let paint dry.

8 Tie a loop of yarn to each of two feathers and hang one from each horn. To hang finished skull, staple a piece of yarn to the back.

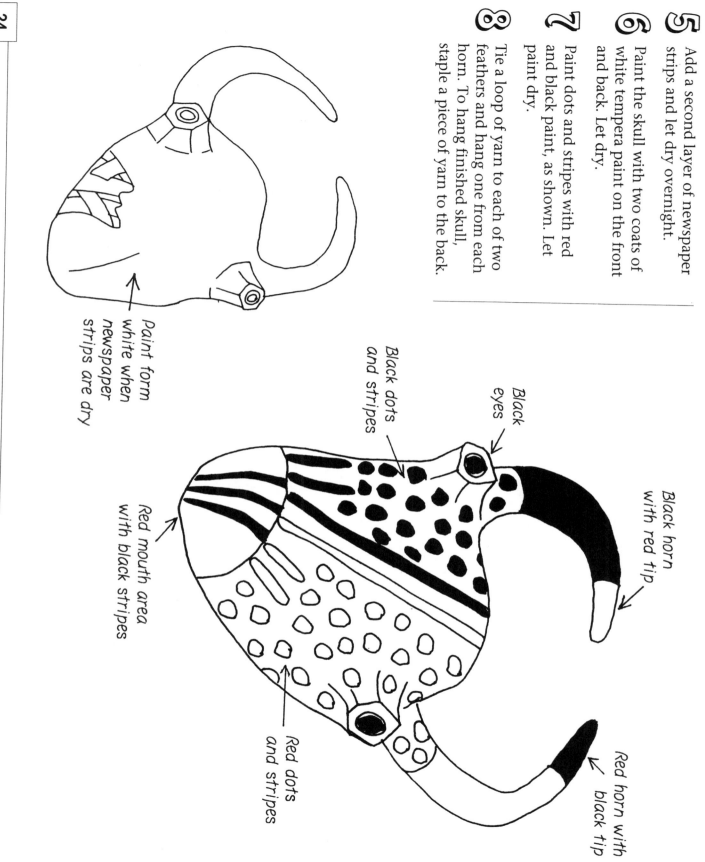

Paint form white when newspaper strips are dry

Black dots and stripes

Black eyes

Black horn with red tip

Red mouth area with black stripes

Red dots and stripes

Red horn with black tip

★ **Cultural Clues** ★

The colors on the Sun Dance Skull had special meaning: black symbolized the earth and red symbolized the people. The dots symbolized their prayers.

Hang yarn loops with feathers

Finished Sun Dance skull

• NATIVE AMERICANS OF NORTH AMERICA •

ESKIMO

INUIT FINGER MASKS

Mask-making is a traditional Inuit craft. Masks are used in ceremonies and Eskimo festivals. Often, women dancers wear little finger masks that are carved out of wood and may have feathers on them. The women wave their hands around during the dance and move to the rhythm of the music.

◆ **MATERIALS** ◆

Pop-top tabs from soda cans (twist them off the cans)

Scrap of light-colored poster board

Glue, markers, pencil, scissors

1. Copy the mask pattern onto the poster board.

2. Draw short lines around the outer edge of the mask, and color the fringe. Draw a funny face on the mask.

3. Cut the fringe. Then, bend it so that one piece is bent toward the front and the next piece is bent toward the back. Alternate all the way around as shown.

4. Turn the mask over and glue the smaller end of the pop-top tab to the back bottom of the mask. Let dry completely.

5. Stick a finger through the hole of the tab and wiggle it. Make enough for several fingers of each hand.

✳ **Cultural Clues** ✳

Alaska became the 49th state to join the United States of America on January 3, 1959.

Cut fringe

Mask

Full-size pattern

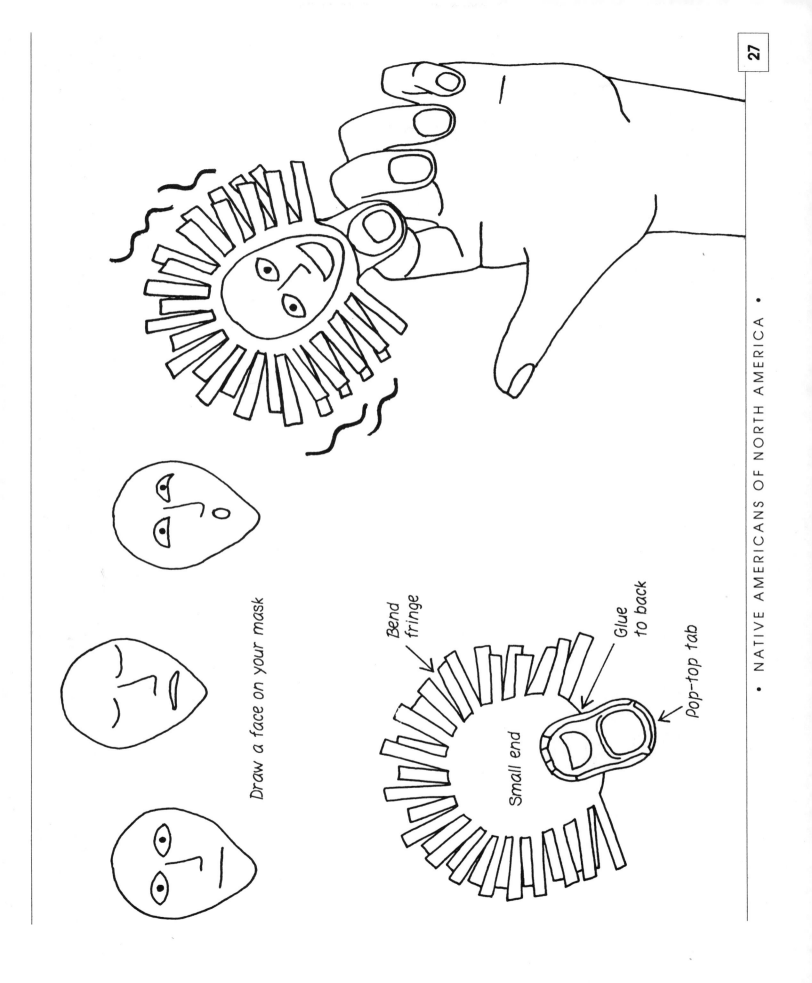

Draw a face on your mask

Bend fringe

Glue to back

Small end

Pop-top tab

ESKiMO LAUGHING MASK

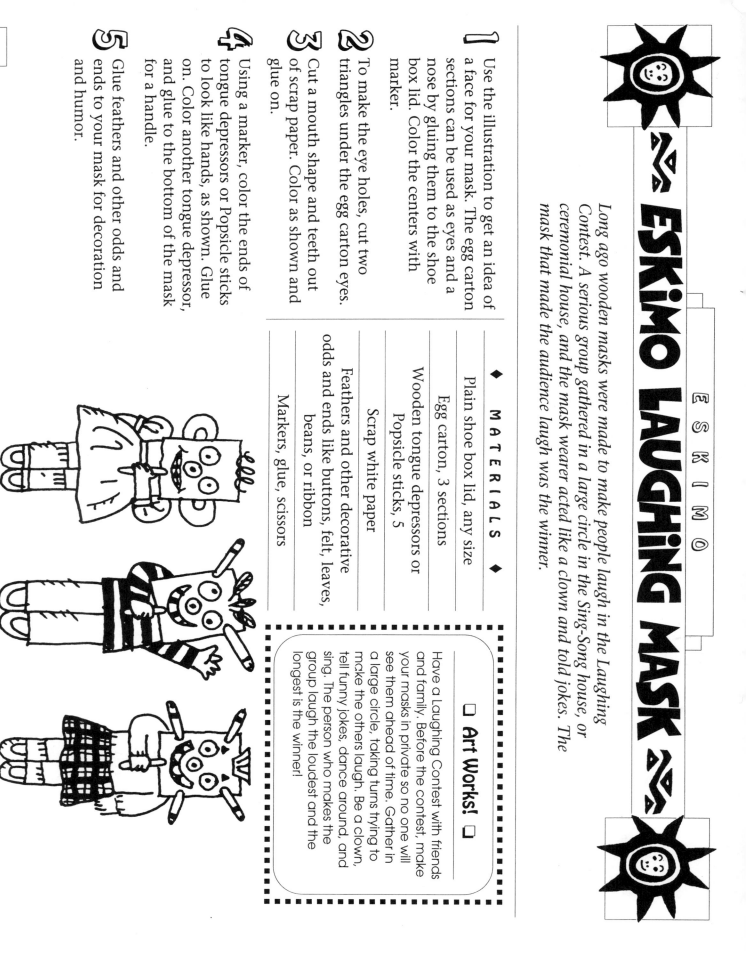

Long ago wooden masks were made to make people laugh in the Laughing Contest. A serious group gathered in a large circle in the Sing-Song house, or ceremonial house, and the mask wearer acted like a clown and told jokes. The mask that made the audience laugh was the winner.

◆ MATERIALS ◆

Plain shoe box lid, any size

Egg carton, 3 sections

Wooden tongue depressors or Popsicle sticks, 5

Scrap white paper

Feathers and other decorative odds and ends like buttons, felt, leaves, beans, or ribbon

Markers, glue, scissors

1 Use the illustration to get an idea of a face for your mask. The egg carton sections can be used as eyes and a nose by gluing them to the shoe box lid. Color the centers with marker.

2 To make the eye holes, cut two triangles under the egg carton eyes.

3 Cut a mouth shape and teeth out of scrap paper. Color as shown and glue on.

4 Using a marker, color the ends of tongue depressors or Popsicle sticks to look like hands, as shown. Glue on. Color another tongue depressor, and glue to the bottom of the mask for a handle.

5 Glue feathers and other odds and ends to your mask for decoration and humor.

☐ Art Works! ☐

Have a Laughing Contest with friends and family. Before the contest, make your masks in private so no one will see them ahead of time. Gather in a large circle, taking turns trying to make the others laugh. Be a clown, tell funny jokes, dance around, and sing. The person who makes the group laugh the loudest and the longest is the winner!

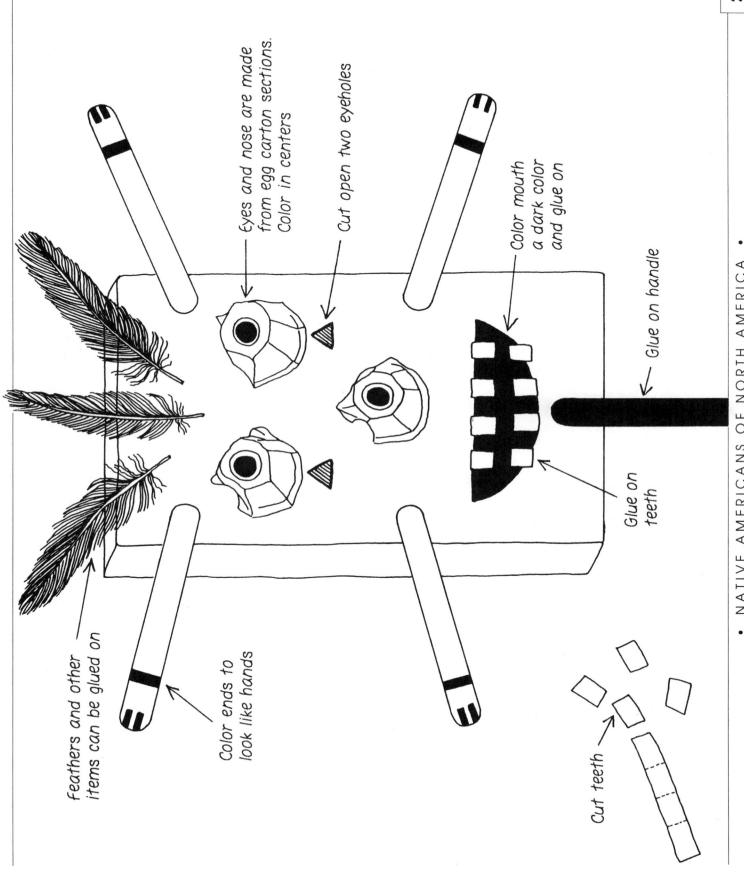

Eyes and nose are made from egg carton sections. Color in centers

Cut open two eyeholes

Color mouth a dark color and glue on

Glue on handle

Glue on teeth

Feathers and other items can be glued on

Color ends to look like hands

Cut teeth

ANIMAL TOTEM POLE

Native Americans of the northwest coast such as the Kwakiutl (Kwa-kee-OO-tul), the Haida (HI-duh), and the Tlingit (TLIN-get) are well known for their totem poles which are hand-carved from large logs. They are usually painted red, black, blue, and green, and often have important animal or spirit designs on them, or may tell a family's history.

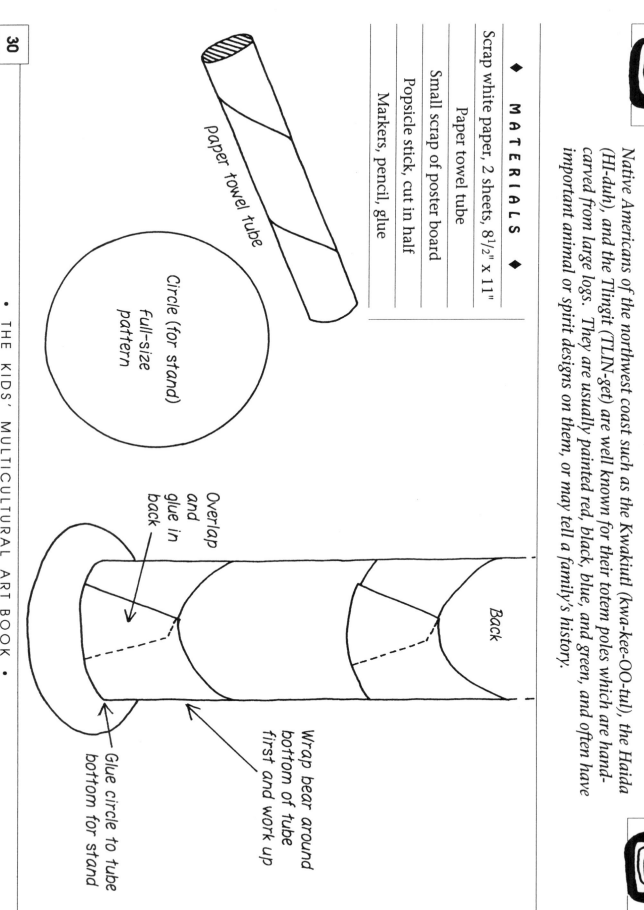

◆ **M A T E R I A L S** ◆

Scrap white paper, 2 sheets, 8½" x 11"

Paper towel tube

Small scrap of poster board

Popsicle stick, cut in half

Markers, pencil, glue

paper towel tube

Circle (for stand)
full-size
pattern

Overlap
and
glue in
back

Wrap bear around
bottom of tube
first and work up

Glue circle to tube
bottom for stand

Back

1. Trace each of the full-size patterns with a pencil, and cut out.

2. Trace the circle onto the poster board, cut out, and glue to the bottom of the paper towel tube.

3. With the markers, color in the bear, wolf, and bird. Draw feathers on the wings with red, black, blue, green, and yellow markers.

4. Starting at the bottom, wrap the bear around the tube. Overlap and glue in the back, as shown.

5. Wrap the wolf above the bear (tuck the feet behind the bear's ears); overlap and glue in the back. Wrap the bird above the wolf (tuck the feet behind the wolf's ears); overlap and glue.

6. Glue the two halves of the Popsicle stick to the back of the bird's wings to keep them from curling up.

✳ Cultural Clues ✳

Some totem poles are so large, they have doorways cut into the bottom that people can walk through! Imagine how big the tree was!

Bear

full-size pattern

Some feather ideas to decorate wings

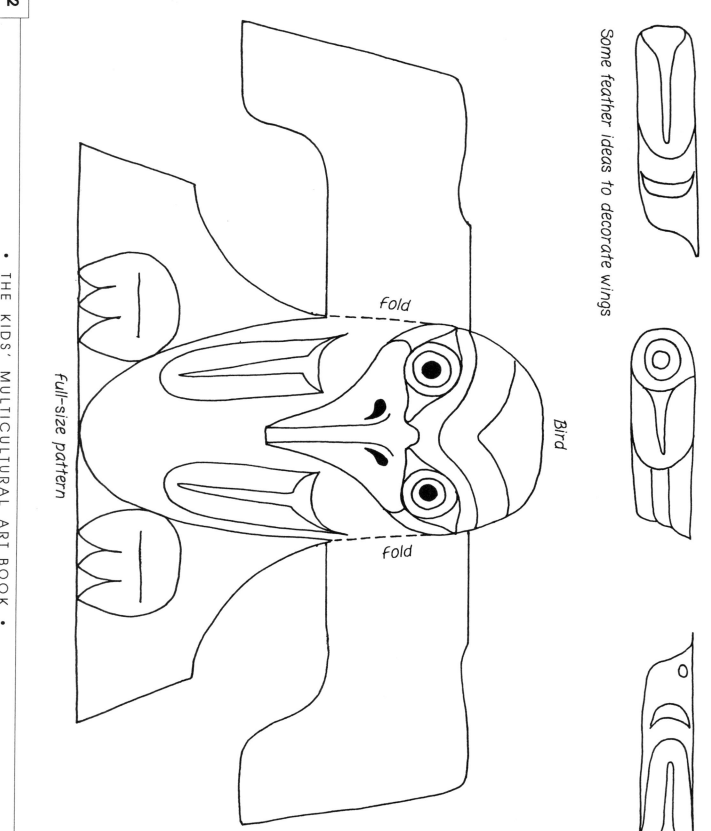

Bird

fold

fold

full-size pattern

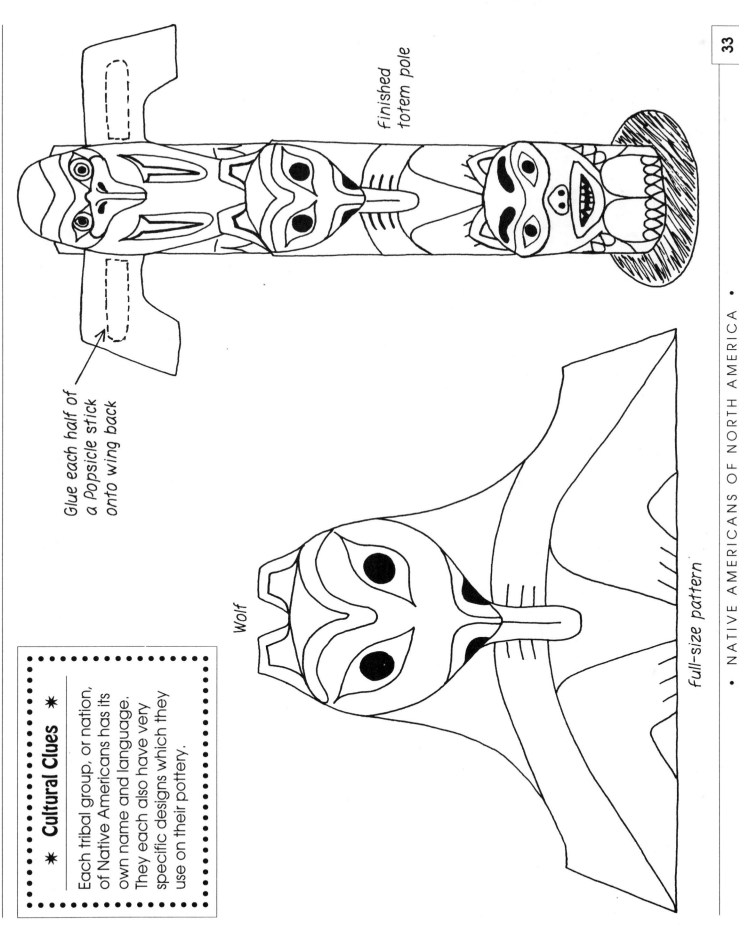

Glue each half of
a Popsicle stick
onto wing back

finished
totem pole

Wolf

full-size pattern

STORYTELLER ANIMAL MASK

The storytellers of the native northwest coast people use many masks to weave their tales. The mask, made of wood painted with rounded, circular, and curvy designs, helps the audience understand who the story is about. Mask carvers often get their ideas from the wild animals around them. In this way, the people live in harmony with nature.

◆ **M A T E R I A L S** ◆

White paper plate, 7"

Wooden tongue depressor or Popsicle stick

Markers, tape, stapler, hole punch, scissors

1 Cut two slits (about 2" in) on each side of the paper plate as shown. Punch two eye holes.

2 Staple and tape the tongue depressor to the inside of the plate at the bottom.

3 Turn the plate over and decorate the plate bottom with markers. Make an animal face.

Paper plate

Cut slits on each side

Punch two eyeholes

Staple and tape on handle

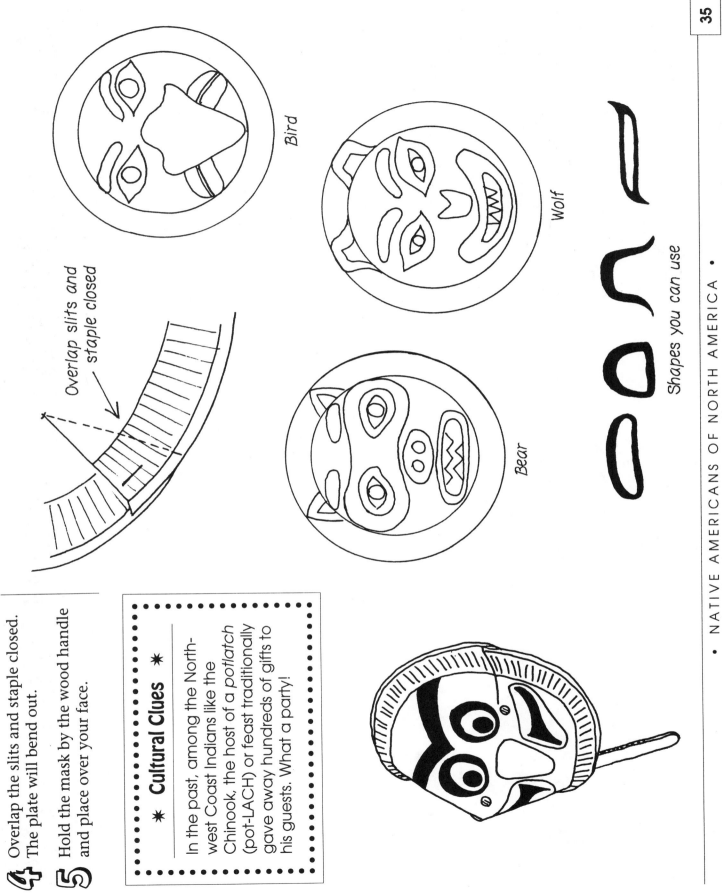

4 Overlap the slits and staple closed. The plate will bend out.

5 Hold the mask by the wood handle and place over your face.

★ Cultural Clues ★

In the past, among the Northwest Coast Indians like the Chinook, the host of a *potlatch* (pot-LACH) or feast traditionally gave away hundreds of gifts to his guests. What a party!

Bird

Wolf

Bear

Shapes you can use

Overlap slits and staple closed

KACHiNA CRADLE DOLL

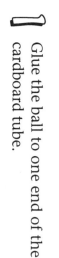
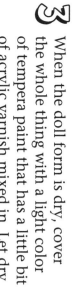
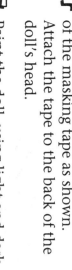

The Hopi (HOPE-ee) and the Zuni (ZOO-nee) of southwest North America believe that spirit kachinas (ka-CHEE-nas), living in the mountains of Arizona, bring water and help the crops grow. There are hundreds of kachinas or spirits in the form of animals, birds, places, and people! Kachina cradle dolls are very simple, with no arms and legs, made from cottonwood and sometimes decorated with feathers. They are hung by a baby's cradle.

1 Glue the ball to one end of the cardboard tube.

2 Apply the newspaper strips and papier-mache paste in a single layer to the complete doll form (tube and ball) as shown on page 152. Let this dry overnight.

3 When the doll form is dry, cover the whole thing with a light color of tempera paint that has a little bit of acrylic varnish mixed in. Let dry.

4 Lay the 3 feathers on the sticky side of the masking tape as shown. Attach the tape to the back of the doll's head.

5 Paint the doll, using light and dark colors, as shown. Let the doll dry.

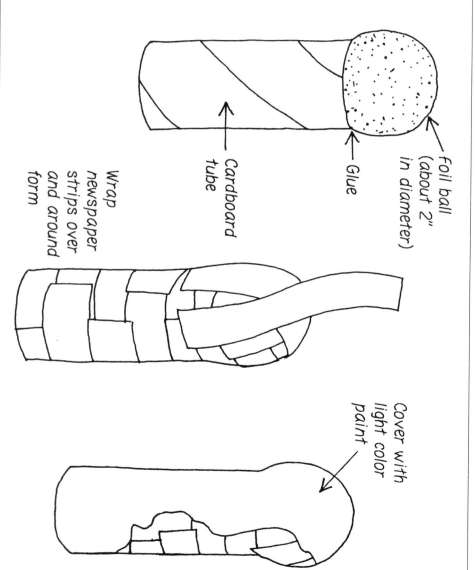

Foil ball (about 2" in diameter)

Glue

Cardboard tube

Wrap newspaper strips over and around form

Cover with light color paint

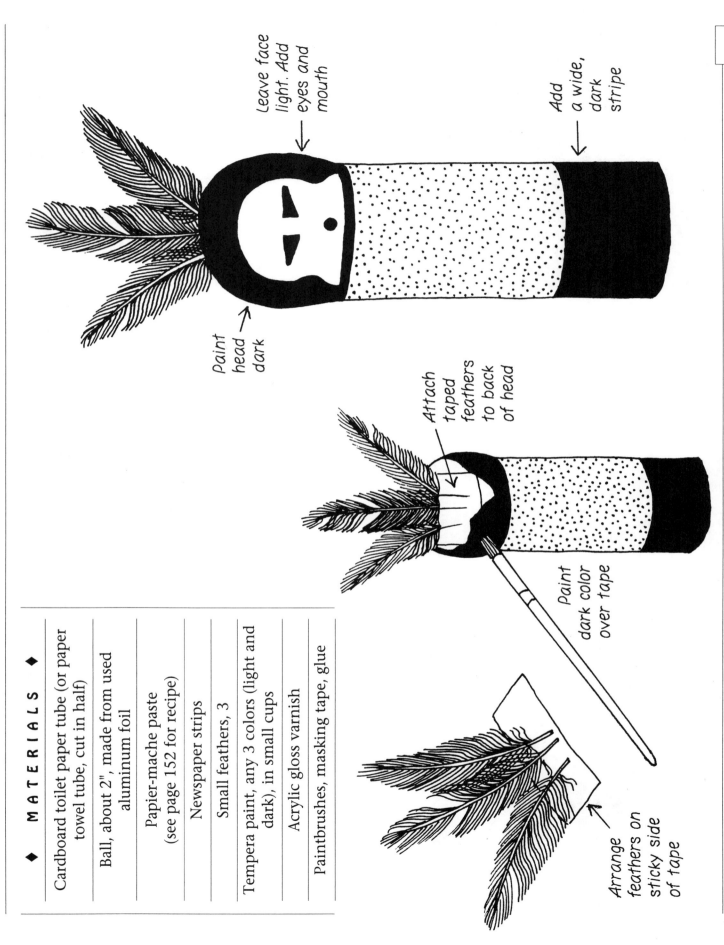

Leave face light. Add eyes and mouth

Paint head dark

Add a wide, dark stripe

Attach taped feathers to back of head

Paint dark color over tape

Arrange feathers on sticky side of tape

◆ **M A T E R I A L S** ◆

Cardboard toilet paper tube (or paper towel tube, cut in half)

Ball, about 2", made from used aluminum foil

Papier-mache paste (see page 152 for recipe)

Newspaper strips

Small feathers, 3

Tempera paint, any 3 colors (light and dark), in small cups

Acrylic gloss varnish

Paintbrushes, masking tape, glue

SOUTHWEST

ZUNI HAND MASK

Many masks are worn during Zuni ceremonies which center around the changing seasons. Sometimes the Zuni masks have a painted human hand on them which is like a signature.

If you save your paper hand mask, you will have a recording of your hand size, and when you are older, you will see how small your hand used to be!

◆ MATERIALS ◆

Scrap paper, about 24" long and 9" wide
Black marker, pencil, clear tape, scissors

1 Trace one of your hands in the middle of the paper. Round out the bottom of your hand shape as shown.

2 Color the hand with black marker. Cut eye holes and a mouth hole, as shown.

3 Make two more hand tracings on each side of the middle hand print, and color black, also. (These will show around the back.)

4 Wrap the paper hand mask around your head, holding the ends in place with your fingers. Lift it off and tape it together. The mask should slip easily over your head and rest on your shoulders.

Trace your hand in the middle

Trace and color in two more hands around back

Tape mask closed

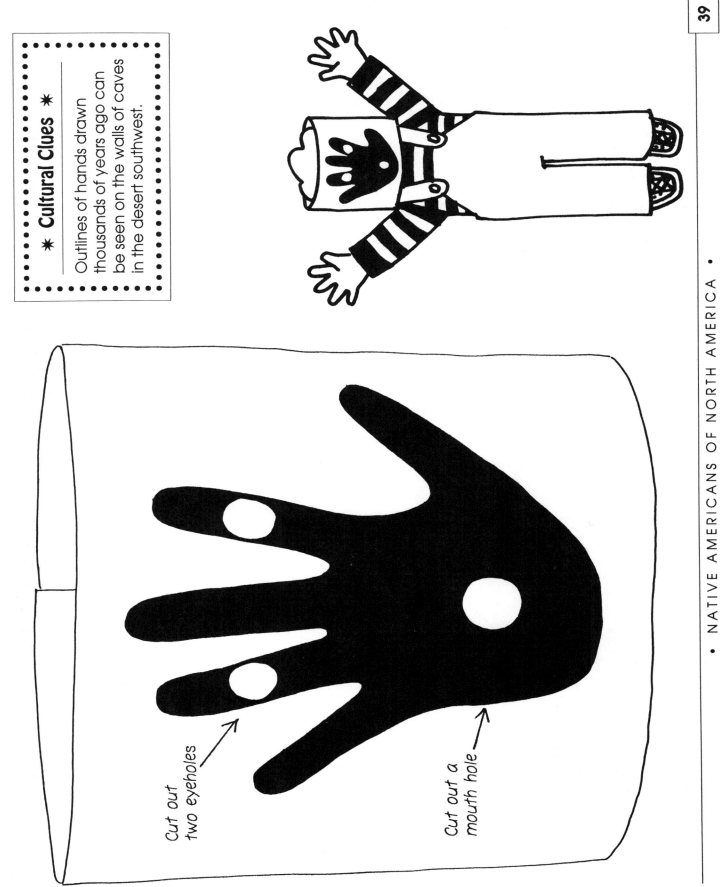

✳ Cultural Clues ✳

Outlines of hands drawn thousands of years ago can be seen on the walls of caves in the desert southwest.

Cut out
two eyeholes

Cut out a
mouth hole

SPONGE PAINTING CUT-OUTS

The Chippewa made cut-outs from white birch bark for patterns to decorate objects. The cut-outs, often of animals, were traced or stencilled on an object such as a mokuk. Cutout patterns were also used on moccasins (shoes) to show where beads would be sewn on. Use your own cut-outs made from poster board to sponge paint designs on notebooks, a tin can, pencil holder, gift wrap, stationery, or art objects you've made.

◆ MATERIALS ◆

Poster board, 14" x 14"

Scrap white paper
(large enough to trace patterns)

Large piece of paper (or object)
for sponge painting

Tempera paint for paper, or acrylic paint
for objects, in small cup

Paper plate, small piece of sponge

Pencil, scissors

1 Trace any cutout pattern shown, or draw your own patterns on the scrap paper. Cut out.

2 Trace the paper patterns onto the poster board, and cut out.

3 Lay the cut-outs on a large piece of paper, or the object you are painting. Put a small curl of masking tape under each cut-out to hold in place as you paint.

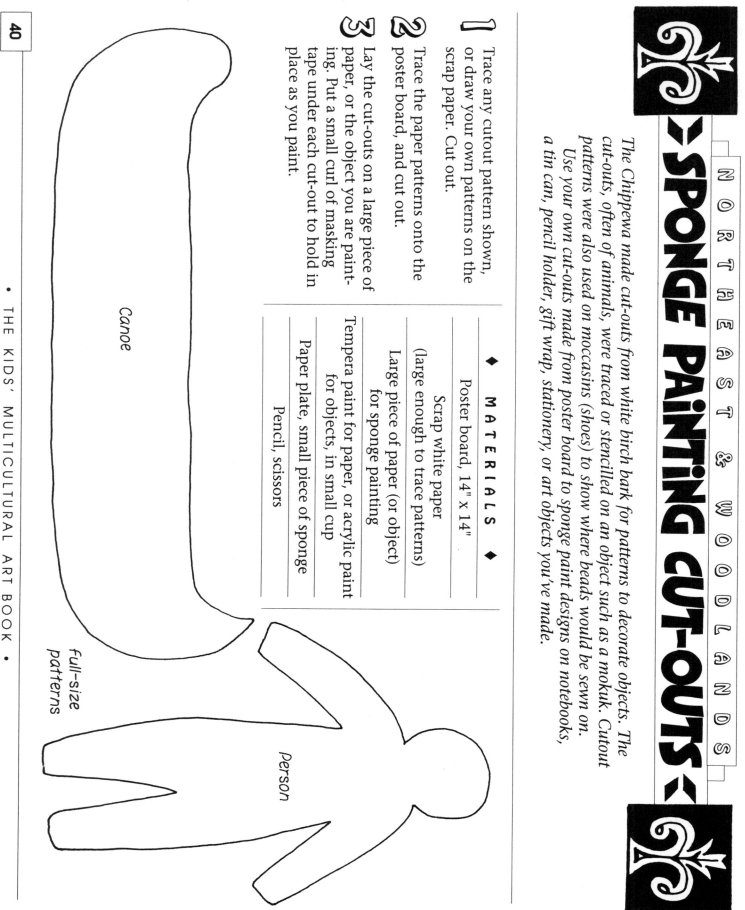

Canoe

full-size
patterns

Person

4 Dip the piece of sponge lightly in the paint, dabbing the sponge all over the paper's (or object's) surface. Dab over the cut-outs.

5 Lift the cut-outs off carefully and the unpainted shapes will appear. Let dry.

Dab paint over cut-outs. Lift off cut-outs carefully

Dip sponge in paint

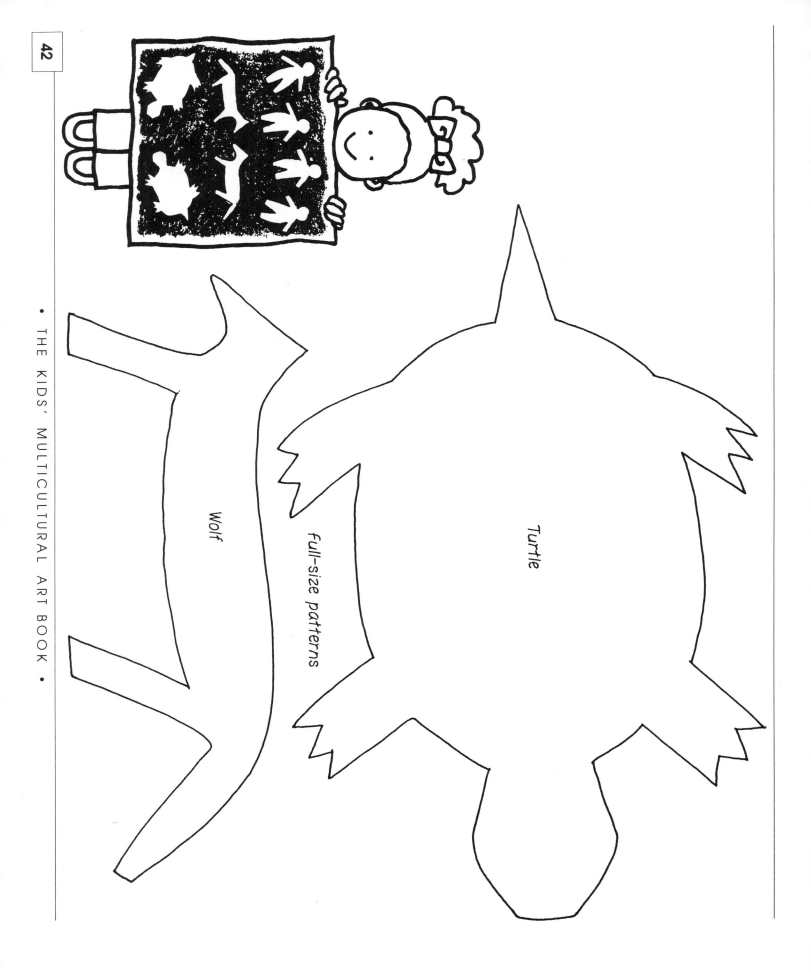

Wolf

Full-size patterns

Turtle

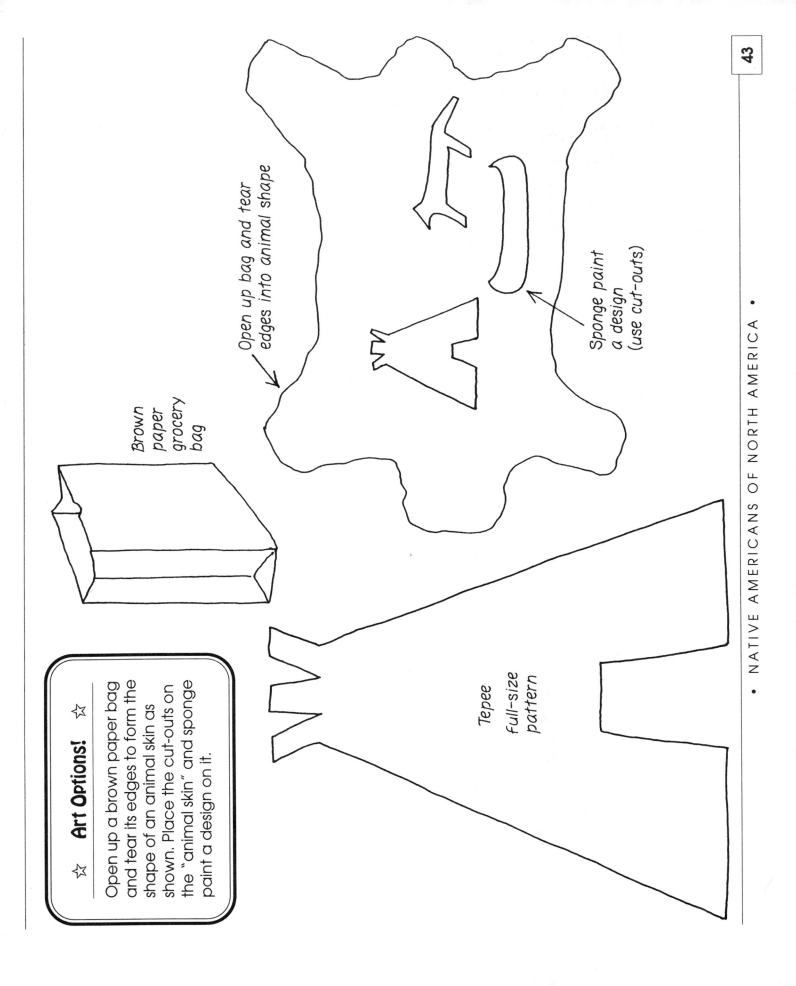

☆ **Art Options!** ☆

Open up a brown paper bag and tear its edges to form the shape of an animal skin as shown. Place the cut-outs on the "animal skin" and sponge paint a design on it.

Brown paper grocery bag

Open up bag and tear edges into animal shape

Sponge paint a design (use cut-outs)

Tepee full-size pattern

CHIPPEWA DREAM CATCHER

The Chippewa, and other Native Americans like the Cherokee, believe good and bad dreams float around at night. They make a dream catcher out of a wood hoop with a web and feathers that hangs above the bed of a newborn baby or a newly married couple. The bad dreams get tangled in the web and disappear when the sun comes up. The good dreams float through the web, down the feather, and onto the sleeping person in bed. Some Chippewa women still make dream catchers.

◆ **M A T E R I A L S** ◆

White paper plate, 9"

Yarn, about 12"

Beads, store-bought or homemade beads (see p. 90)

Feather

Masking tape, pencil, scissors, hole punch

1 Draw a large ring inside the rim of a paper plate.

2 Cut out the center of the plate to the inner edge of ring. Then, cut off the outside rim of the plate, leaving the ring.

3 Punch about 16 holes around the ring.

Cut off outside rim of plate.

Cut out center of plate

Punch about 16 holes around remaining ring

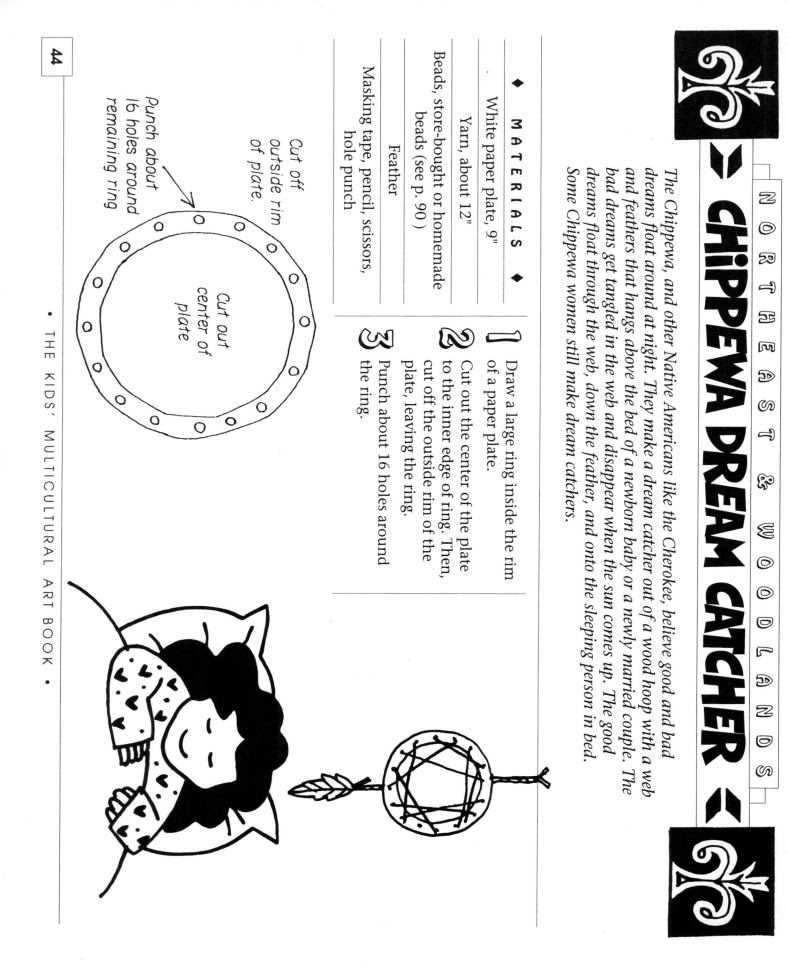

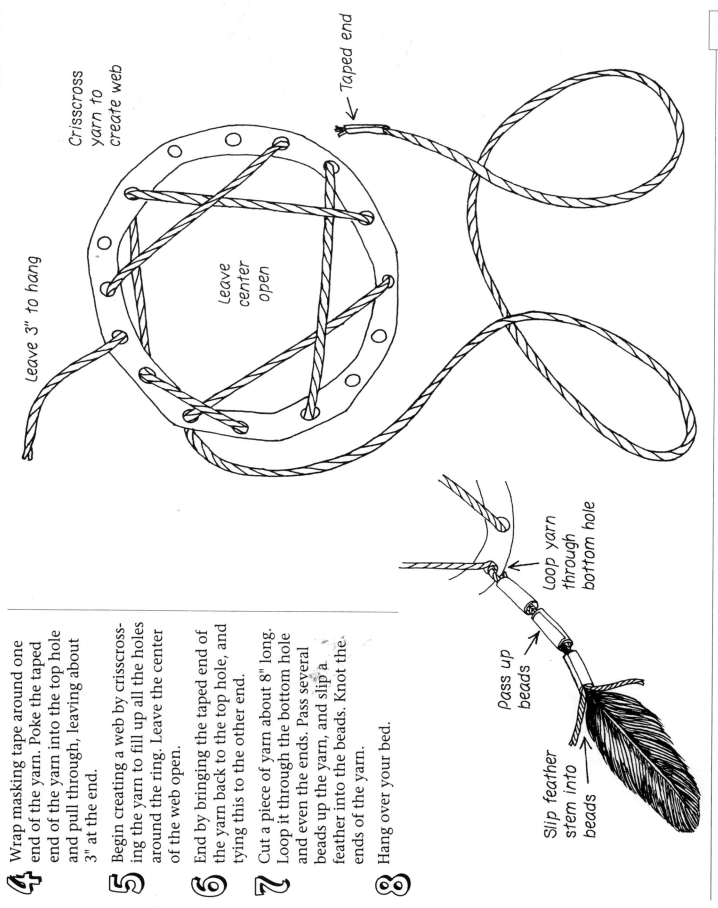

Crisscross yarn to create web

Leave 3" to hang

Leave center open

Taped end

Loop yarn through bottom hole

Pass up beads

Slip feather stem into beads

4. Wrap masking tape around one end of the yarn. Poke the taped end of the yarn into the top hole and pull through, leaving about 3" at the end.

5. Begin creating a web by crisscrossing the yarn to fill up all the holes around the ring. Leave the center of the web open.

6. End by bringing the taped end of the yarn back to the top hole, and tying this to the other end.

7. Cut a piece of yarn about 8" long. Loop it through the bottom hole and even the ends. Pass several beads up the yarn, and slip a feather into the beads. Knot the ends of the yarn.

8. Hang over your bed.

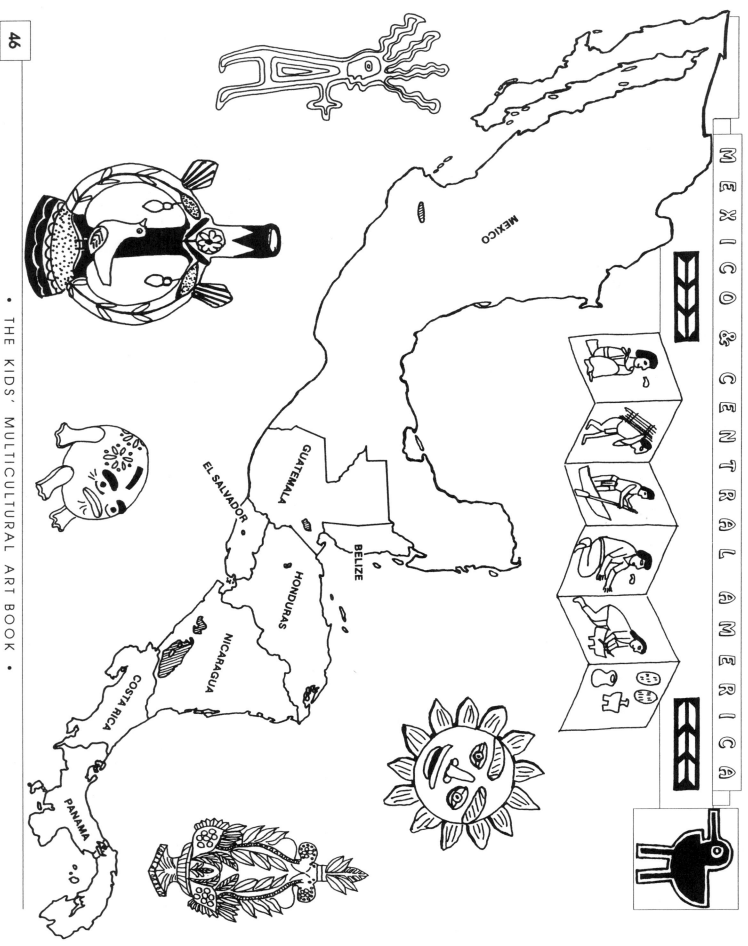

MEXICO & CENTRAL AMERICA

MEXICO

GUATEMALA

BELIZE

EL SALVADOR

HONDURAS

NICARAGUA

COSTA RICA

PANAMA

HISPANICS

MEXICO & CENTRAL AMERICA

Mexico and Central America are a perfect example of what happens when cultures slowly — over hundreds and hundreds of years — blend together. You see, Mexico and Central America had their own native Indians. The natives were from two great civilizations, the Aztec and the Maya. Then, at about the same time that the English were settling in North America, peoples from Spain began settling in Mexico and Central America. Over many hundreds of years, they joined with the Spaniards and a wonderful new ethnic group, called Hispanics, evolved, drawing on all three backgrounds — the Aztec, the Mayan, and the Spanish. If you ever get to visit this part of the world, you will find the Hispanic culture overflowing with the excitement of this amazing joining of peoples. The world is a far richer place for what these cultures have given us.

Have you ever eaten an enchilada? Do you wear vibrant-colored woven Guatemalan belts or sweaters? Have you tried to break open a piñata full of candy? Well, then, you've already experienced some of the fun and excitement of cultural sharing! In Mexico and Central America, children and adults enjoy many different types of crafts, including weaving, pottery, and painting. The weavers use wool and cotton threads to make lovely blankets and sweaters, among other items. Potters create beautiful clay objects, such as plates and bowls. Some of these crafts are created for everyday use; others are simply for decoration.

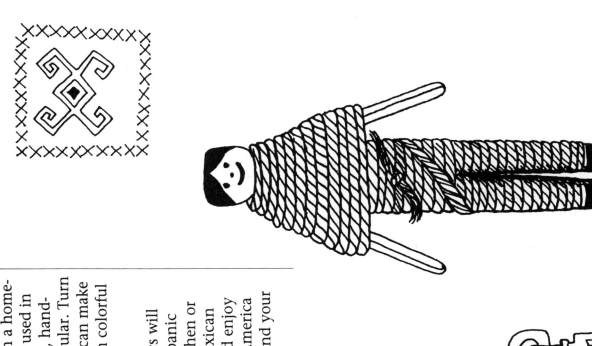

You, too, can share in the fun and pride of Mexican and Central American arts and crafts, using simple materials found right in your own home. Making your own Guatemala-inspired *Green Toad Bank* or *Mexican Tree of Life* are only two of the many projects you can do to experience the richness of these countries.

In Guatemala, a central American country that borders Mexico, potters make plates with beautiful designs painted on them. You can create your own authentic plate designs using paper plates and tempera paint. Or, weave your own

placemats or wall hanging with a home-made loom similar to the kind used in Central America. In Costa Rica, handsomely decorated carts are popular. Turn to page 72 and learn how you can make a *Costa Rican Cart* — filled with colorful paper flowers!

Turn to page 72 and learn how you can make a *Costa Rican Cart*

These projects and many others will help you experience these Hispanic cultures right in your own kitchen or play room. So put on some Mexican music, roll up your sleeves, and enjoy a part of Mexico and Central America with crayons, paper, paint — and your imagination, of course!

AZTEC SUN GOD

The sun is an important theme in Mexican and Central American arts and crafts. The Aztecs, who lived in Mexico from about 1300 to 1500, carved a huge Sun Stone that functioned as a type of calendar. Clay suns are still made in Mexico in a place called Metepec by the Nahua Indians, who are descendants of the Aztecs.

1 Trace the circle pattern onto scrap paper and cut out.

2 Roll out a ball of salt dough on a wooden board or piece of wax paper.

3 Press the pattern gently onto the dough slab, and cut out. Roll extra dough into a ball.

4 Remove the pattern and move the dough circle to a cookie sheet. If it loses its shape, wet your fingers and reshape it.

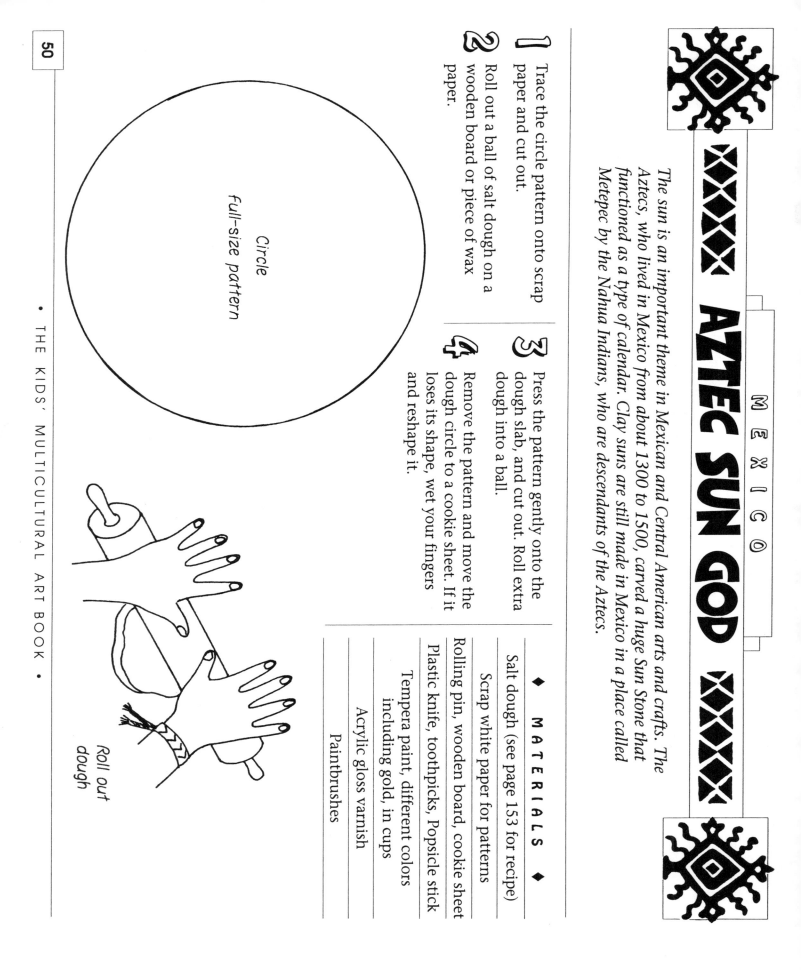

Circle
full-size pattern

Roll out
dough

◆ **MATERIALS** ◆

Salt dough (see page 153 for recipe)

Scrap white paper for patterns

Rolling pin, wooden board, cookie sheet

Plastic knife, toothpicks, Popsicle stick

Tempera paint, different colors including gold, in cups

Acrylic gloss varnish

Paintbrushes

5 To decorate, roll out another slab and a coil from the extra dough. Cut out triangular or other shapes to make the sun's rays, eyes, eyebrows, mouth, tongue, and anything else you want to add to the face.

6 Connect the shapes by pressing gently with wet fingers. Smooth all edges down. (A Popsicle stick makes a good tool for smoothing and connecting dough pieces.)

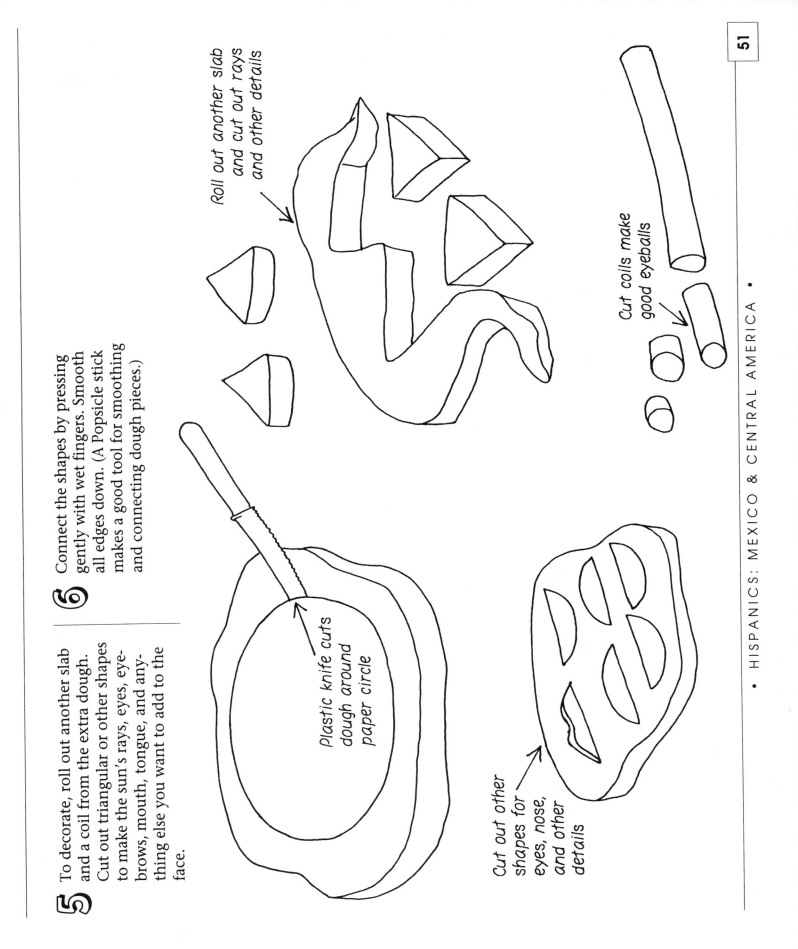

Roll out another slab and cut out rays and other details

Cut coils make good eyeballs

Plastic knife cuts dough around paper circle

Cut out other shapes for eyes, nose, and other details

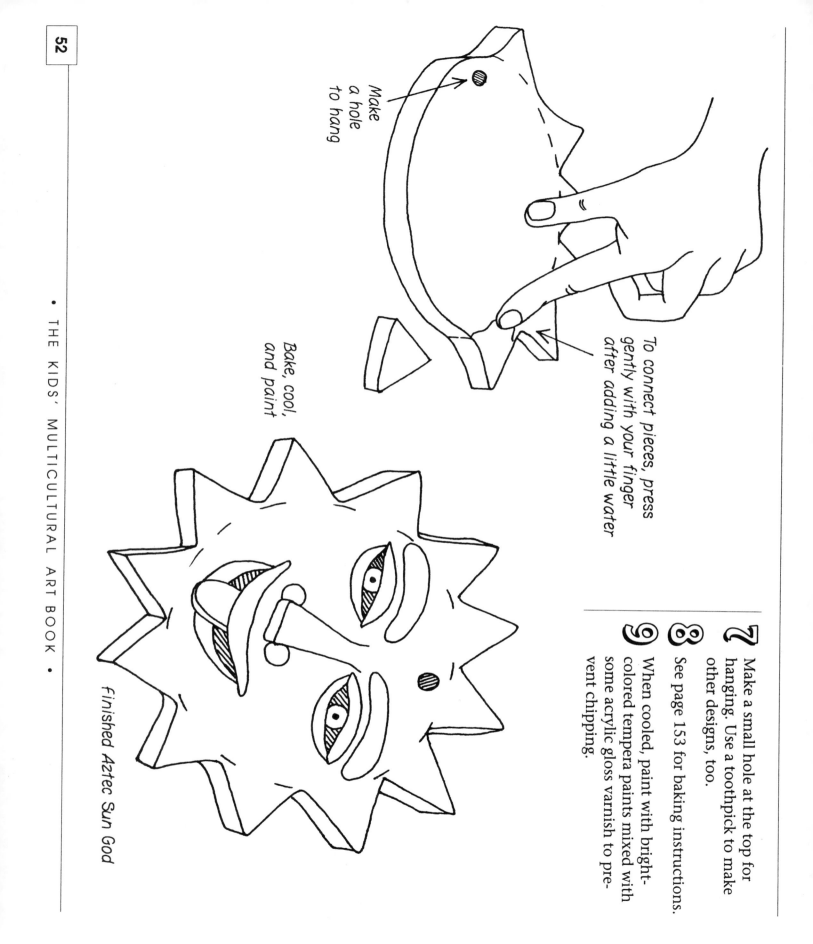

Make
a hole
to hang

To connect pieces, press
gently with your finger
after adding a little water

Bake, cool,
and paint

finished Aztec Sun God

7 Make a small hole at the top for
hanging. Use a toothpick to make
other designs, too.

8 See page 153 for baking instructions.

9 When cooled, paint with bright-
colored tempera paints mixed with
some acrylic gloss varnish to pre-
vent chipping.

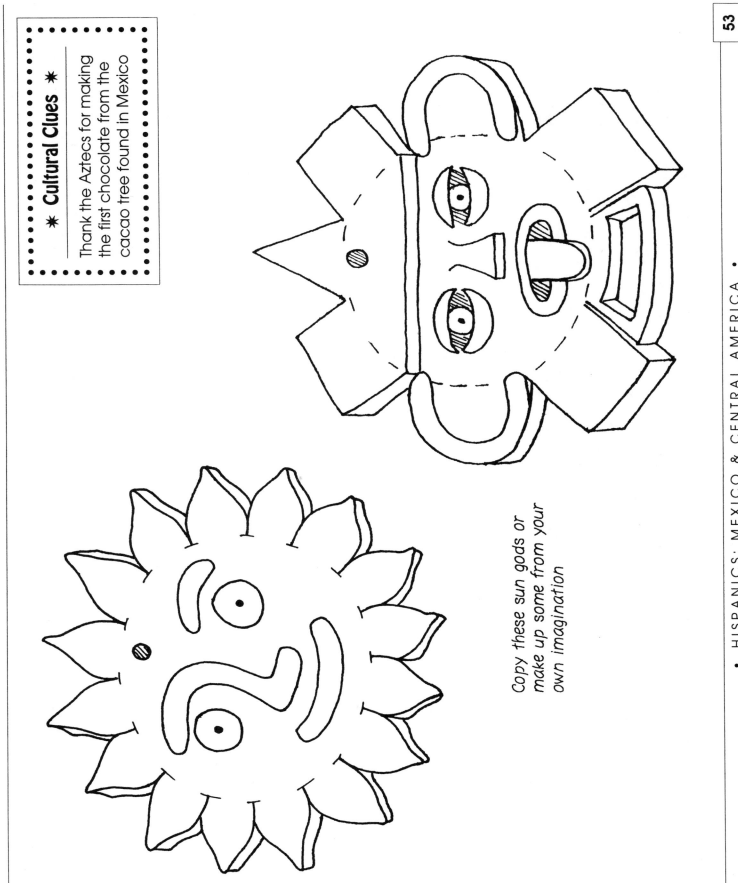

✳ Cultural Clues ✳

Thank the Aztecs for making the first chocolate from the cacao tree found in Mexico

Copy these sun gods or make up some from your own imagination

MEXICO

AZTEC CODEX

A codex, or fold-out picture book, written by an Aztec scribe, or writer, often contained a record of history, calendars, gods, and daily life of the Aztec people with interesting pictures and symbols. Make your own codex with drawings, photos, or even pressed flowers.

◆ MATERIALS ◆

White paper, 8 1/2" x 11", 2 sheets

White poster board, 5" x 6", 2 pieces

Stencils

Markers, pencil, glue, scissors

1 Fold both sheets of white paper in half the long way. Cut each piece in half on the fold, making four long, narrow sheets.

2 Now, fold in half the short way.

3 Glue all four sheets by overlapping the edges as shown.

4 Now, glue the end pieces of the long folded paper to a 5" x 6" piece of poster board to make book covers. The book should fold out accordion-style.

5 Decorate your fold-out picture book any way you wish. You can make a counting book with stencils, as shown, or glue on pictures, write poems, or illustrate a story about your pet.

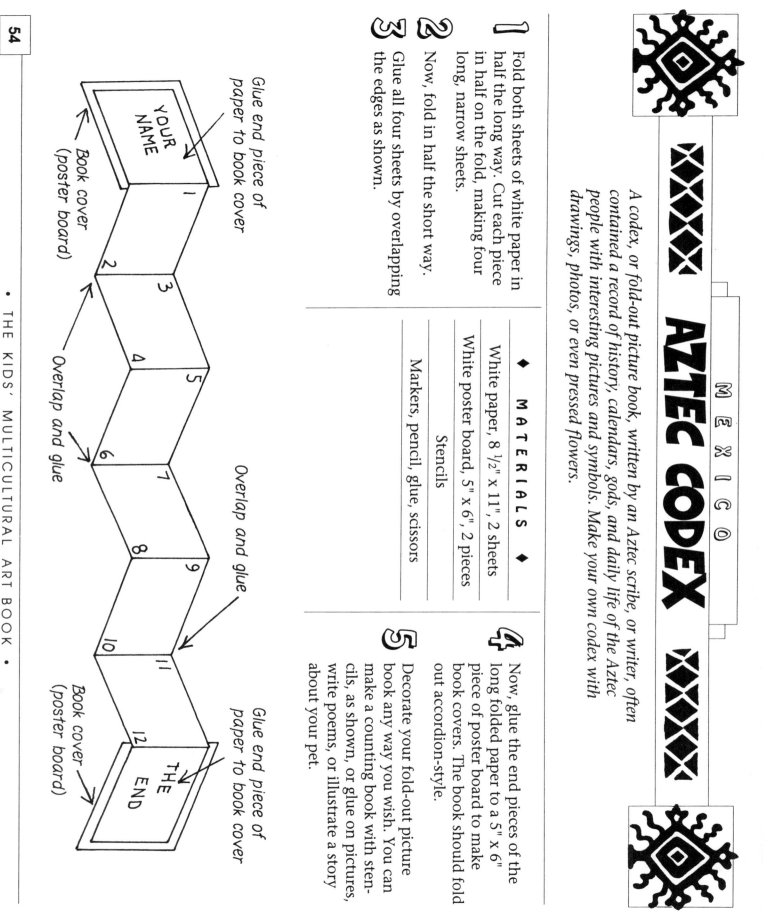

Glue end piece of paper to book cover

Book cover (poster board)

YOUR NAME

Overlap and glue

Overlap and glue

Book cover (poster board)

Glue end piece of paper to book cover

THE END

Decorate your fold-out picture book (codex) any way you like. Here is one idea

front cover

My Counting Book

Spine

Overlap and glue

5

3

4

6

Overlap and glue

HUICHOL YARN ART

Many people around the world buy yarn paintings of the Huichol (WEE-chol) Indians of northwest Mexico because of the brilliant colors and interesting designs that tell stories about their history and religion. A yarn painting is made by pressing yarn into beeswax that has been warmed by the sun.

◆ **M A T E R I A L S** ◆

Yarn, many colors

Paper bowl

Glue, Popsicle stick, tape

Scrap cardboard, any size

To make Yarn Art Bowl:

1   Swirl glue on the inside bottom of the paper bowl.

2   Take the end of a long length of yarn and begin wrapping it in a circular pattern, using the Popsicle stick to pat the yarn in place. Go around and around. Add more glue and start another color yarn. Keep going around the inside of the bowl until you reach the rim. Be patient.

3   Flip the bowl over and swirl glue in a circle on the outside bottom of the bowl. Wrap yarn around in a circular pattern until you reach the outer rim of the bowl. When one color runs out, start another.

4   Flip the bowl back over. Use a piece of yarn to finish off the rim of the bowl. Let this dry.

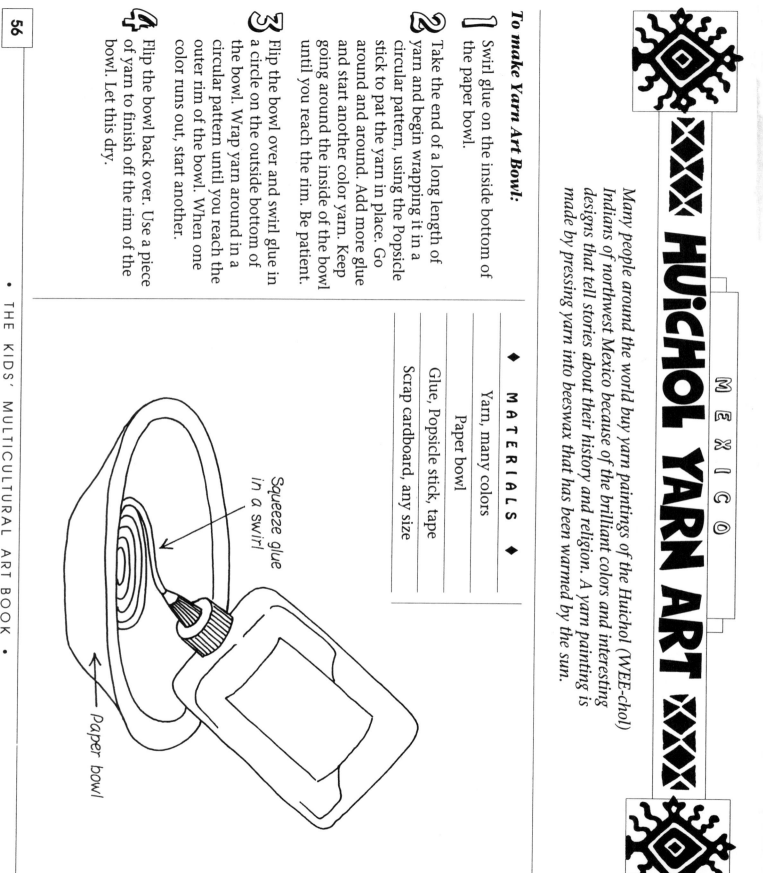

Squeeze glue
in a swirl

Paper bowl

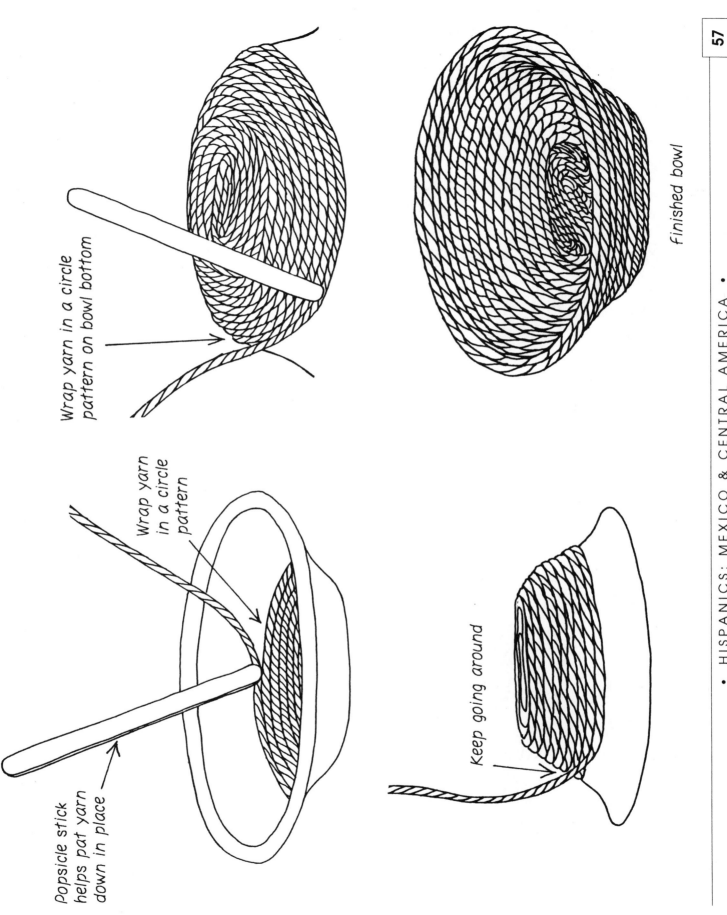

Popsicle stick
helps pat yarn
down in place

Wrap yarn
in a circle
pattern

Keep going around

Wrap yarn in a circle
pattern on bowl bottom

finished bowl

To make Yarn Art Hanging Picture:

1. Start with a scrap piece of cardboard. Squeeze out a bead of glue into a design you wish. Birds, people, fish, deer and the sun are just some of the designs the Huichol Indians use. Make up your own if you wish.

2. Take the end of a long length of yarn and begin pressing it onto the glue. Use a Popsicle stick to help press the yarn in place.

3. Switch colors and fill up the whole surface of the cardboard with yarn, including the background of your designs. Let this dry.

4. Glue or tape a small piece of yarn to the back of the cardboard to hang your yarn art.

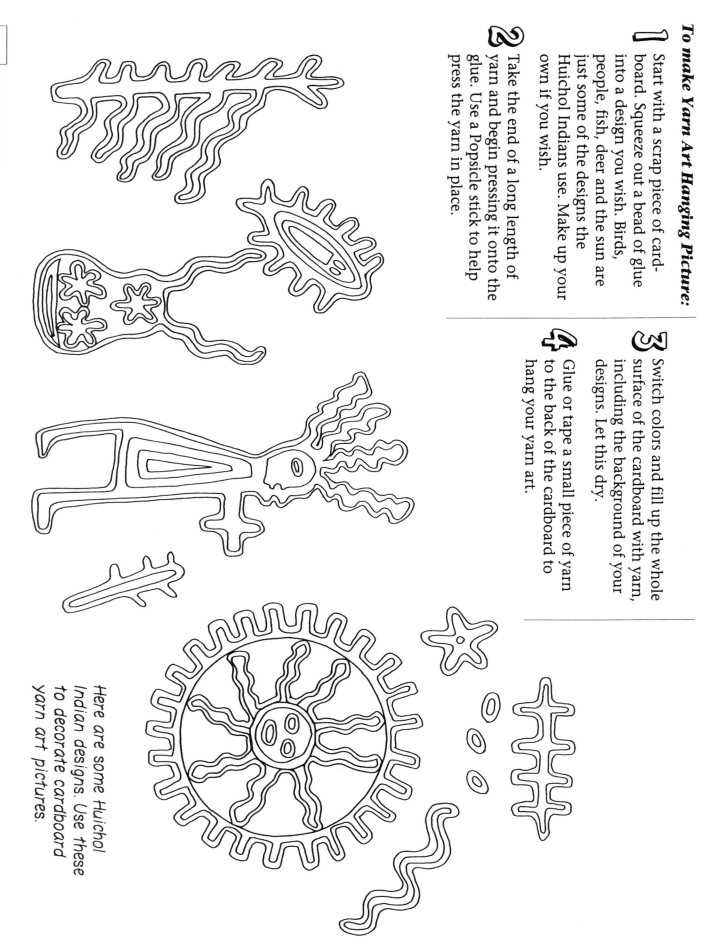

Here are some Huichol Indian designs. Use these to decorate cardboard yarn art pictures.

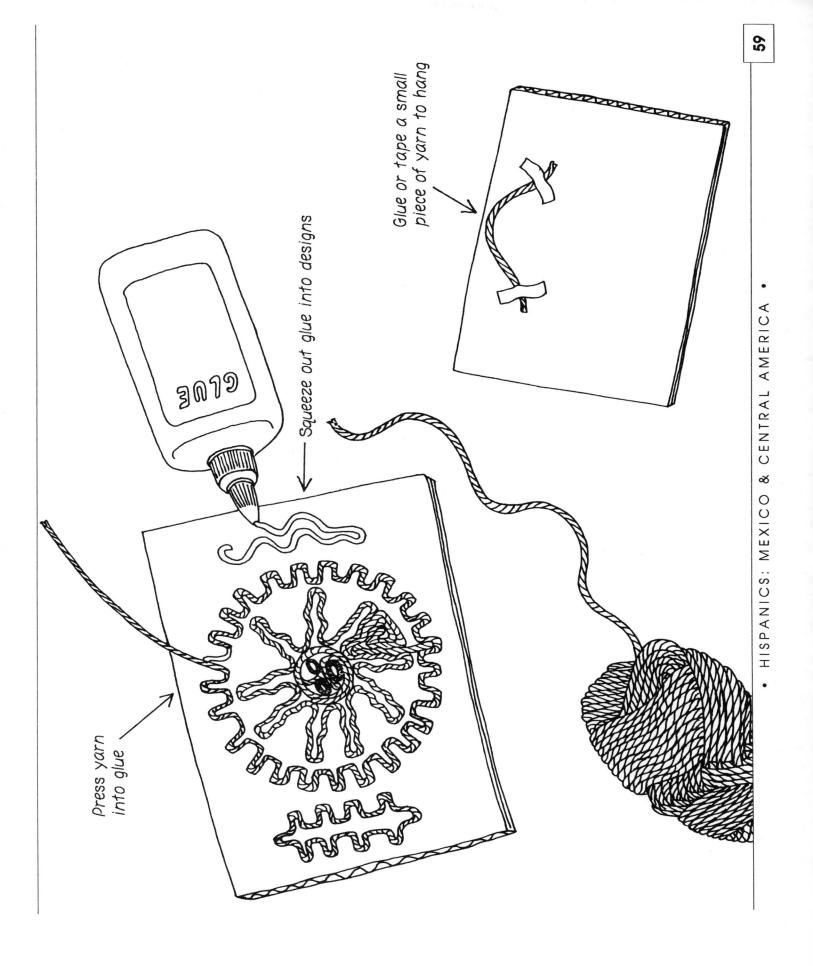

Press yarn
into glue

GLUE

Squeeze out glue into designs

Glue or tape a small
piece of yarn to hang

MEXICAN TIN ROOSTER

Mexican tin art — so popular today — dates from the 1500s. Today, tin candlesticks, plates, frames, and many other useful and beautiful objects, are usually hand-tinted in bright colors.

◆ MATERIALS ◆

Aluminum pie plate, 8" or 9"

Scrap paper

Markers, ballpoint pen, pencil, scissors, stapler

1. Cut away the sides of the pie plate. To form a stand, take about a 5" piece of the pie plate's side and overlap the two ends together, keeping the plate's folded edge on the bottom. Staple in two places.

2. Trace the rooster pattern onto scrap paper, cut out, and trace pattern onto the pie plate circle with a ballpoint pen. Press the pen into the tin very lightly to create "etched-in" designs for feathers, dots, and other details. The more detail you give it, the better it will look.

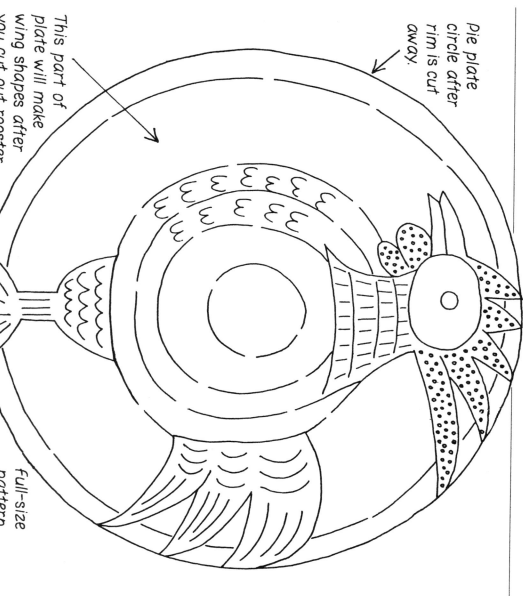

Pie plate circle after rim is cut away.

This part of plate will make wing shapes after you cut out rooster

Full-size pattern

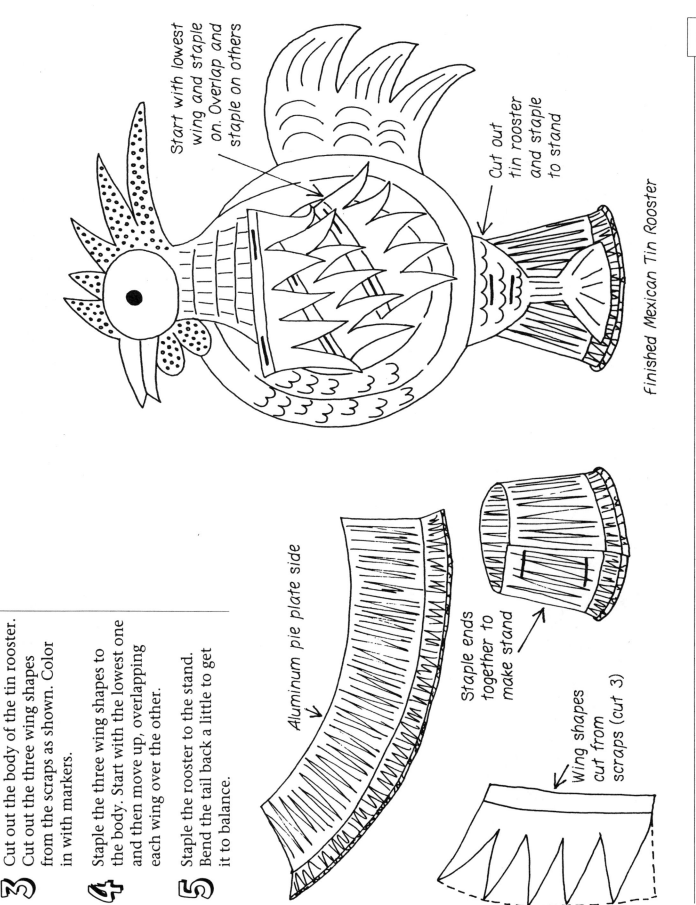

3 Cut out the body of the tin rooster. Cut out the three wing shapes from the scraps as shown. Color in with markers.

4 Staple the three wing shapes to the body. Start with the lowest one and then move up, overlapping each wing over the other.

5 Staple the rooster to the stand. Bend the tail back a little to get it to balance.

Start with lowest wing and staple on. Overlap and staple on others

Cut out tin rooster and staple to stand

Finished Mexican Tin Rooster

Aluminum pie plate side

Staple ends together to make stand

Wing shapes cut from scraps (cut 3)

MEXICO

FOLK ART TREE OF LiFE

The Tree of Life is one of the most beautiful and interesting folk art objects made in Mexico. Traditionally, it is made from clay in the shape of a tree and can be decorated with branches, leaves, fruits, vines, flowers, birds, animals, and people. Some are used as decoration, and others are used in Mexican villages for ceremonies; some are large, and others are small.

You can make a Tree of Life from papier-mache and some other inexpensive materials around the house. Listen to some music from Mexico while you work.

◆ **M A T E R I A L S** ◆

Papier-mache paste (see page 152 for recipe) in bowl

Newspaper strips

Paper towel tube, paper bowl (to be used as base)

Recycled aluminum foil, cardboard (small scrap), 2 paper clips

Acrylic or tempera paints, any colors you wish, in small cups

Acrylic gloss varnish

Paintbrushes, masking tape, scissors

1 Flip the paper bowl over and tape the paper towel tube on top of it.

2 Shape two pieces of aluminum foil about 8" long into two coils for the branches. Tape the coils to the bowl and the top of the paper tube as shown.

3 Shape an 8" piece of aluminum foil into a bird with your hands. Tape the bird onto the base or anywhere you like.

4 Cut two (or more) leaf shapes from the cardboard scrap and tape to the tops of the branches.

Shape a bird out of aluminum foil

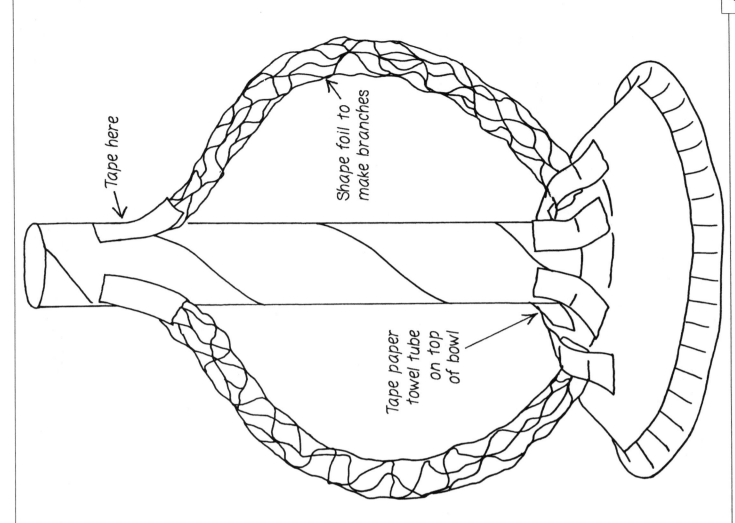

Tape here

Shape foil to make branches

Tape paper towel tube on top of bowl

5 Follow instructions on page 152 to cover entire sculpture and base with papier-mache paste and newspaper. Let dry overnight. Add a second layer and let dry.

6 To add fruits to the branches, open up paper clips, stick the hooked ends into the branches, and wrap papier-mache-dipped strips around the bottom ends of as many paper clips as you like.

7 When completely dry, paint on leaves, squiggly lines, flowers, and any other details. The more color you use, the better. Let this dry. (If you use tempera paints, add a little acrylic gloss varnish to them before painting.)

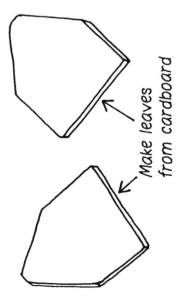

Make leaves from cardboard

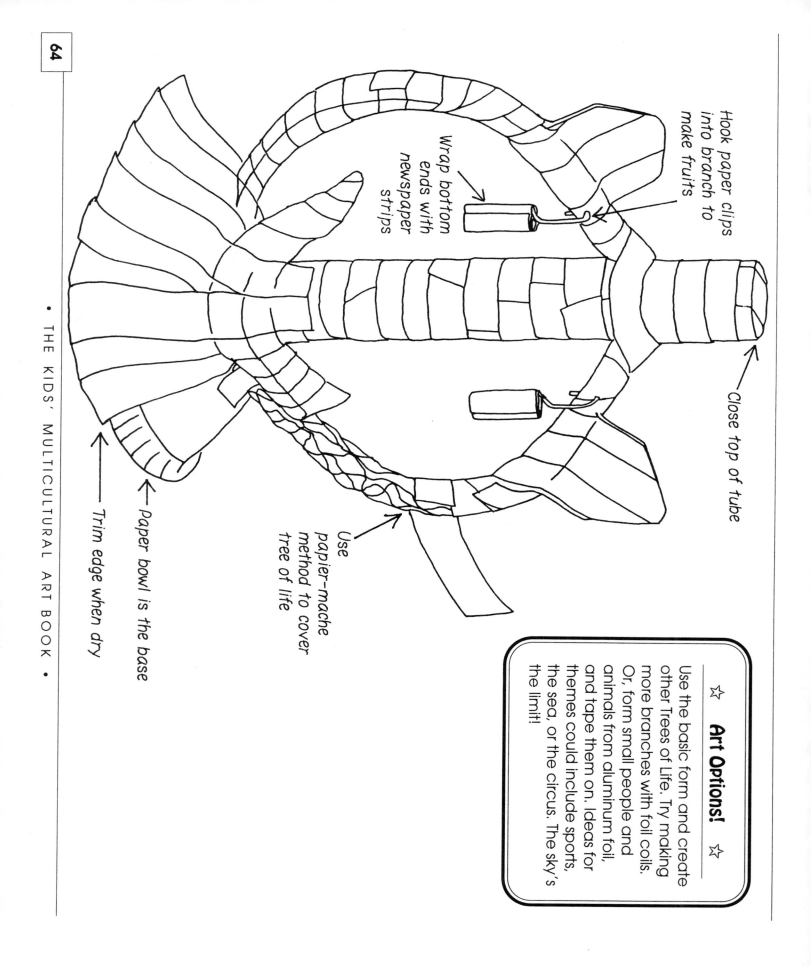

Hook paper clips
into branch to
make fruits

Wrap bottom
ends with
newspaper
strips

Close top of tube

Use
papier-mache
method to cover
tree of life

Paper bowl is the base

Trim edge when dry

☆ **Art Options!** ☆

Use the basic form and create
other Trees of Life. Try making
more branches with foil coils.
Or, form small people and
animals from aluminum foil,
and tape them on. Ideas for
themes could include sports,
the sea, or the circus. The sky's
the limit!

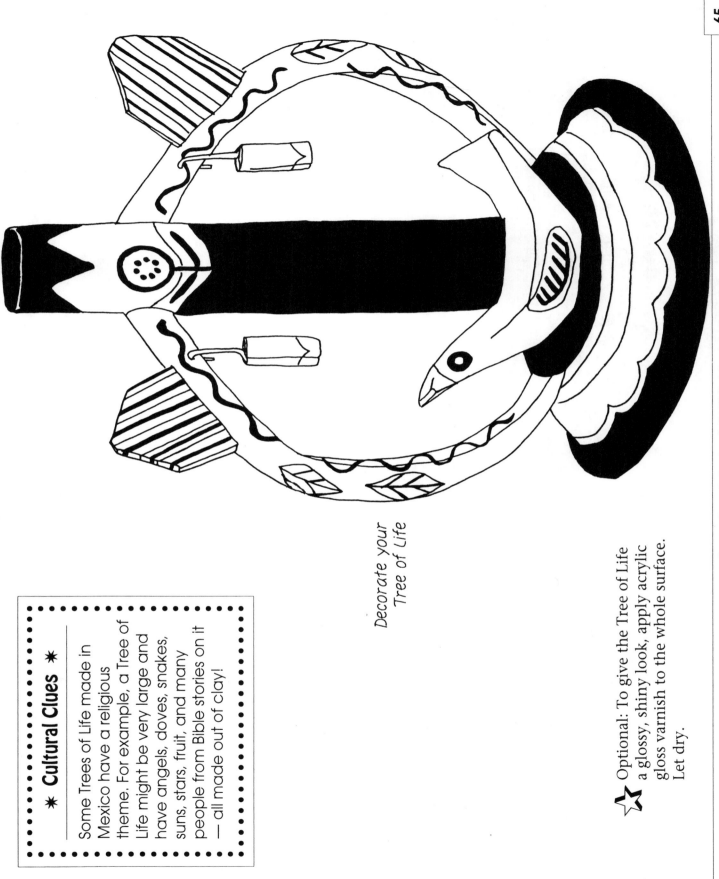

Decorate your
Tree of Life

☆ Optional: To give the Tree of Life a glossy, shiny look, apply acrylic gloss varnish to the whole surface. Let dry.

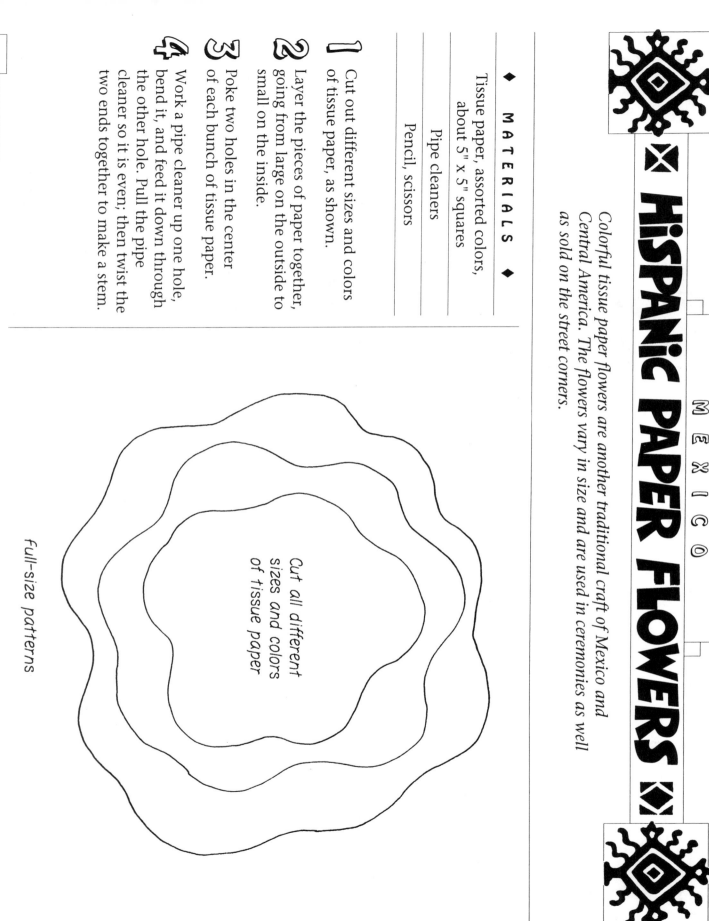

MEXICO

HISPANIC PAPER FLOWERS

Colorful tissue paper flowers are another traditional craft of Mexico and Central America. The flowers vary in size and are used in ceremonies as well as sold on the street corners.

◆ MATERIALS ◆

Tissue paper, assorted colors, about 5" x 5" squares

Pipe cleaners

Pencil, scissors

1 Cut out different sizes and colors of tissue paper, as shown.

2 Layer the pieces of paper together, going from large on the outside to small on the inside.

3 Poke two holes in the center of each bunch of tissue paper.

4 Work a pipe cleaner up one hole, bend it, and feed it down through the other hole. Pull the pipe cleaner so it is even; then twist the two ends together to make a stem.

Cut all different sizes and colors of tissue paper

full-size patterns

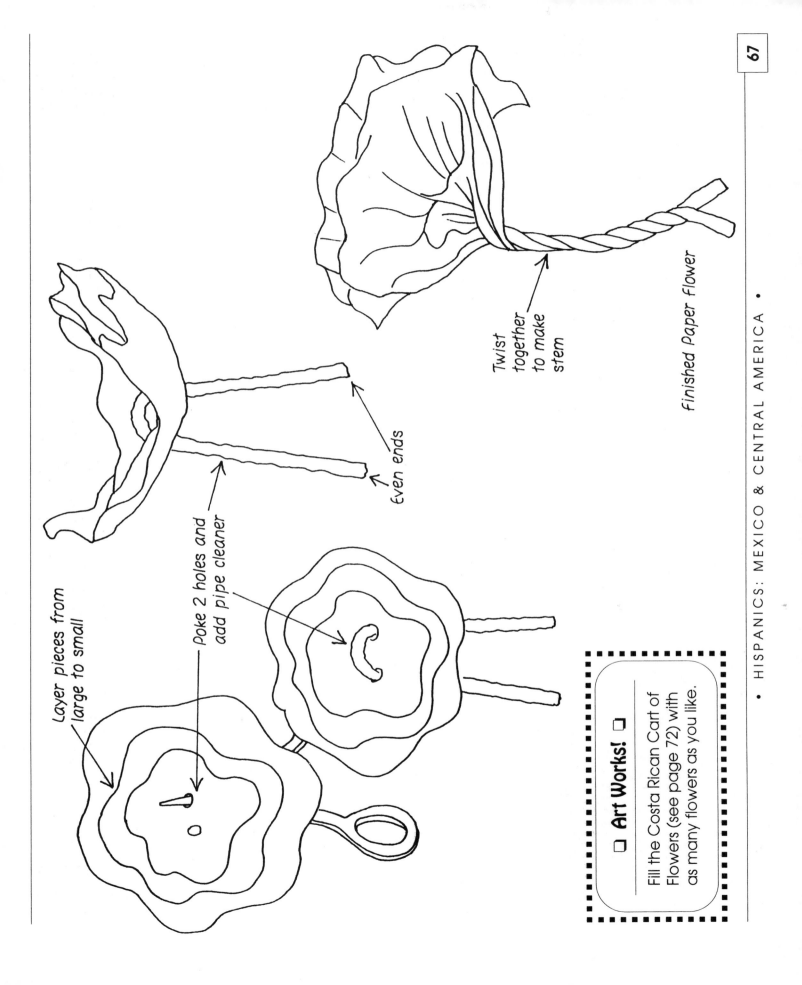

Layer pieces from large to small

Poke 2 holes and add pipe cleaner

Even ends

Twist together to make stem

Finished Paper Flower

□ **Art Works!** □

Fill the Costa Rican Cart of Flowers (see page 72) with as many flowers as you like.

CARDBOARD LOOM WEAVING

The weavers of Central America and Mexico join threads together on looms to make cotton and wool blankets, clothing, bags, belts, and beautiful wall hangings. In Guatemala, weavers use bird and animal designs to make their colorful creations even more beautiful. Using a simple cardboard loom and your imagination, experiment with different colors and types of yarn to create your one-of-a-kind weaving.

◆ M A T E R I A L S ◆

Cardboard, about 5" x 6"

Yarn, different colors

Scissors

Wind yarn around cardboard to form loom

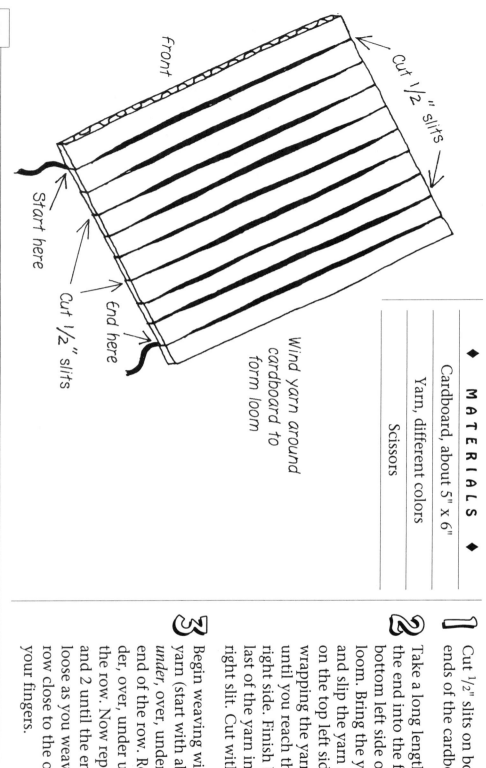

Cut 1/2" slits

front

Start here

End here

Cut 1/2" slits

1. Cut 1/2" slits on both of the short ends of the cardboard.

2. Take a long length of yarn and slip the end into the first slit on the bottom left side of the cardboard loom. Bring the yarn up to the top and slip the yarn into the first slit on the top left side. Continue wrapping the yarn top to bottom, until you reach the end on the right side. Finish by slipping the last of the yarn into the bottom right slit. Cut with scissors.

3. Begin weaving with long lengths of yarn (start with about 2'). Row 1 is under, over, under, over until the end of the row. Row 2 is over, under, over, under until the end of the row. Now repeat from Rows 1 and 2 until the end. Keep the yarn loose as you weave, but push each row close to the one before it with your fingers.

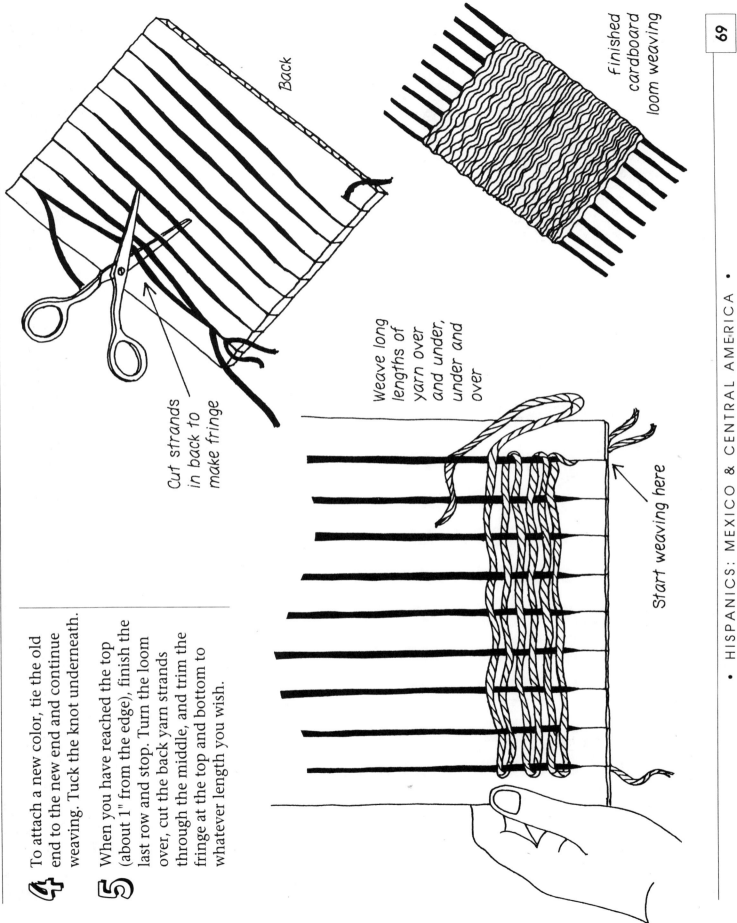

4 To attach a new color, tie the old end to the new end and continue weaving. Tuck the knot underneath.

5 When you have reached the top (about 1" from the edge), finish the last row and stop. Turn the loom over, cut the back yarn strands through the middle, and trim the fringe at the top and bottom to whatever length you wish.

Back

Cut strands in back to make fringe

finished cardboard loom weaving

Weave long lengths of yarn over and under, under and over

Start weaving here

CENTRAL AMERICA

WORRY DOLL

The children of Central America tell their troubles and worries before going to bed to tiny dolls made of colorful threads — one doll for each worry. The child places the dolls under a pillow, and, while asleep, the worry dolls solve all the problems! This worry doll is a little larger than those made in Central America.

◆ MATERIALS ◆

Wooden doll pin (available at most arts and crafts stores), or straight clothespin

Popsicle stick

Yarn, any colors

Scissors, markers, pencil, glue, masking tape

1 Cut the Popsicle stick to make the arms as shown. You won't need the middle piece.

2 Glue the arms to the sides of the doll pin. Wrap a piece of masking tape around this and let it dry for at least two hours (overnight is best). Remove the tape when dry.

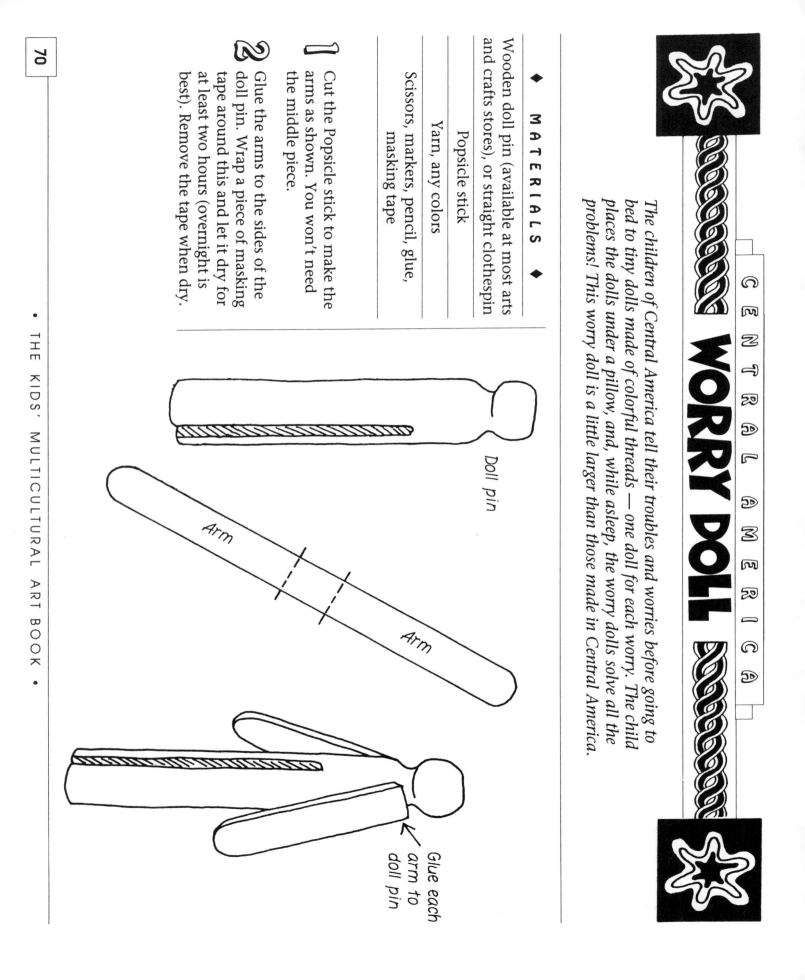

Doll pin

Arm

Arm

Glue each arm to doll pin

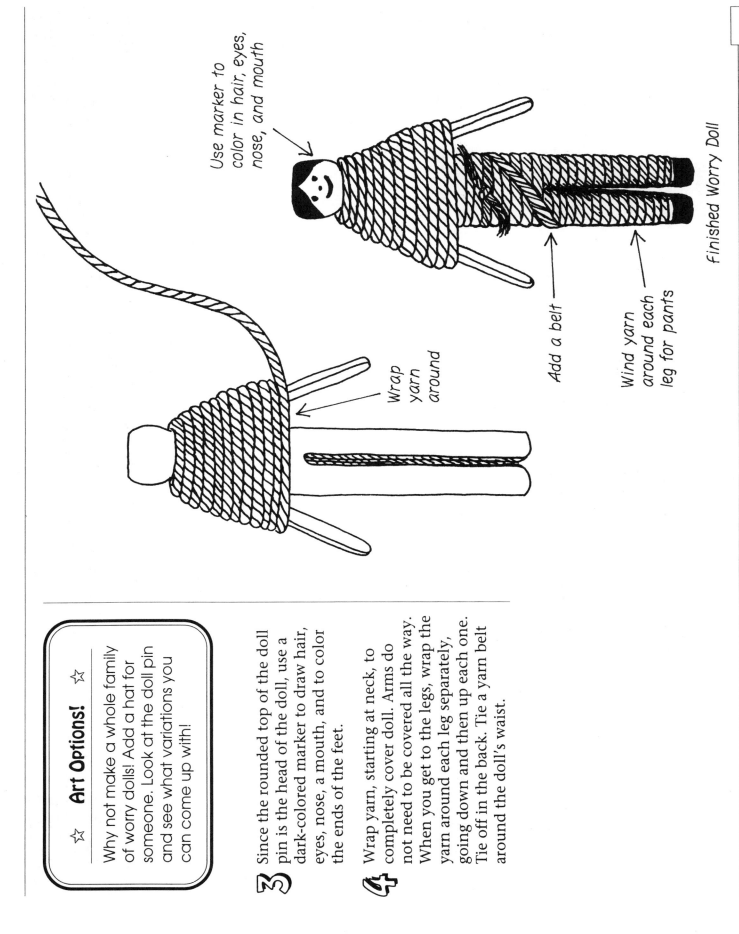

Use marker to color in hair, eyes, nose, and mouth

Finished Worry Doll

Add a belt

Wind yarn around each leg for pants

Wrap yarn around

☆ Art Options! ☆

Why not make a whole family of worry dolls! Add a hat for someone. Look at the doll pin and see what variations you can come up with!

3 Since the rounded top of the doll pin is the head of the doll, use a dark-colored marker to draw hair, eyes, nose, a mouth, and to color the ends of the feet.

4 Wrap yarn, starting at neck, to completely cover doll. Arms do not need to be covered all the way. When you get to the legs, wrap the yarn around each leg separately, going down and then up each one. Tie off in the back. Tie a yarn belt around the doll's waist.

COSTA RICAN CART

On Columbus's fourth voyage to the New World, he visited a land that he thought was full of riches and gold, so he named it Costa Rica, or gold coast. Today, Costa Rican craftspeople create famous painted wooden ox carts, each made carefully by hand and decorated with beautiful designs of leaves and flowers.

Shoe box without lid, small to medium size

Cardboard, 12" x 12", or big enough to fit wheel pattern four times

Paper fasteners, 4

◆ M A T E R I A L S ◆

Gesso (available at arts and crafts stores) or white latex house paint

Tempera paint in many bright colors

Scrap paper, newspaper

Paintbrushes, pencil, scissors

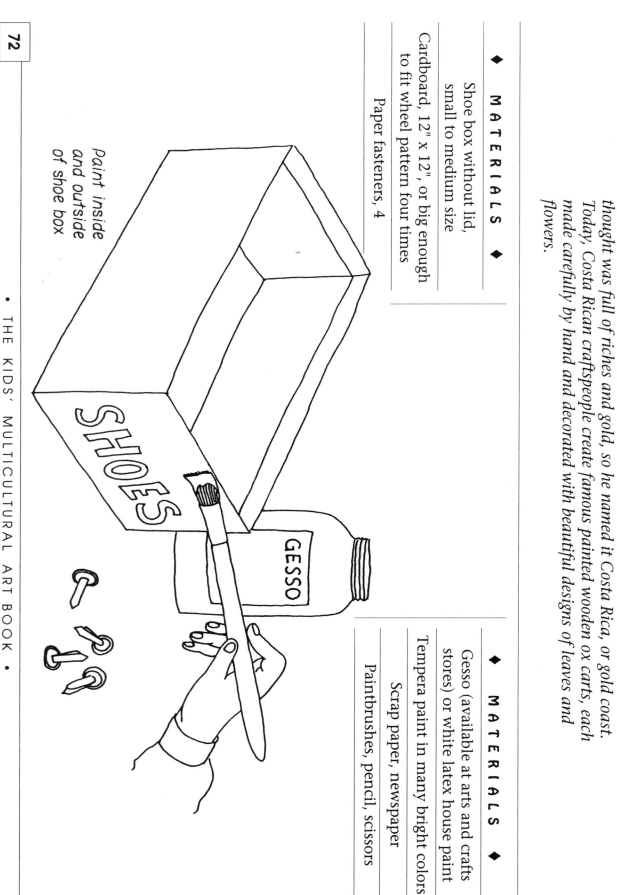

Paint inside and outside of shoe box

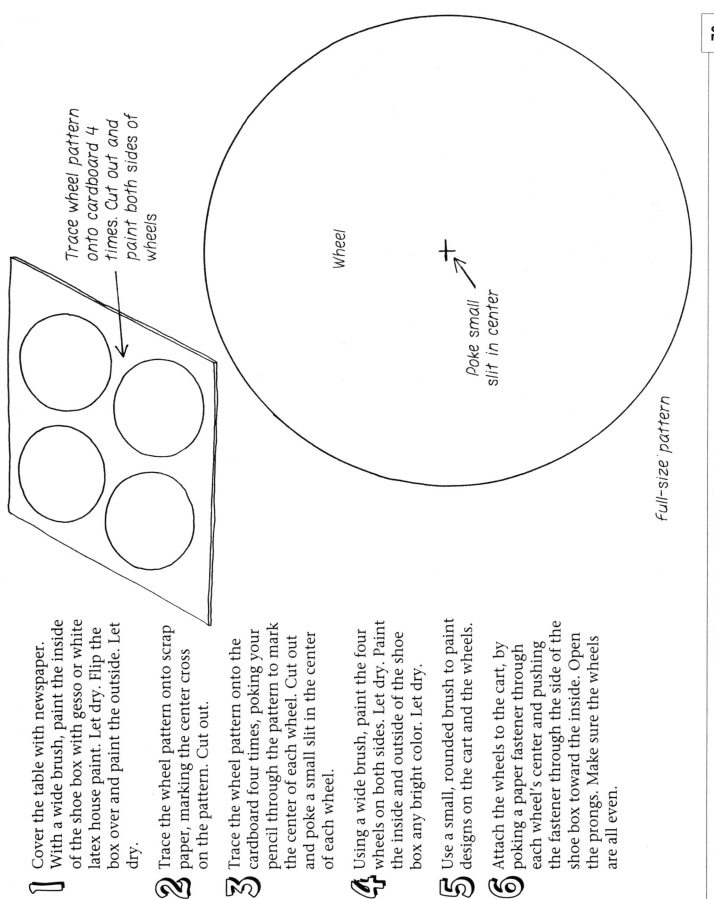

Trace wheel pattern onto cardboard 4 times. Cut out and paint both sides of wheels

Wheel

Poke small slit in center

full-size pattern

1. Cover the table with newspaper. With a wide brush, paint the inside of the shoe box with gesso or white latex house paint. Let dry. Flip the box over and paint the outside. Let dry.

2. Trace the wheel pattern onto scrap paper, marking the center cross on the pattern. Cut out.

3. Trace the wheel pattern onto the cardboard four times, poking your pencil through the pattern to mark the center of each wheel. Cut out and poke a small slit in the center of each wheel.

4. Using a wide brush, paint the four wheels on both sides. Let dry. Paint the inside and outside of the shoe box any bright color. Let dry.

5. Use a small, rounded brush to paint designs on the cart and the wheels.

6. Attach the wheels to the cart, by poking a paper fastener through each wheel's center and pushing the fastener through the side of the shoe box toward the inside. Open the prongs. Make sure the wheels are all even.

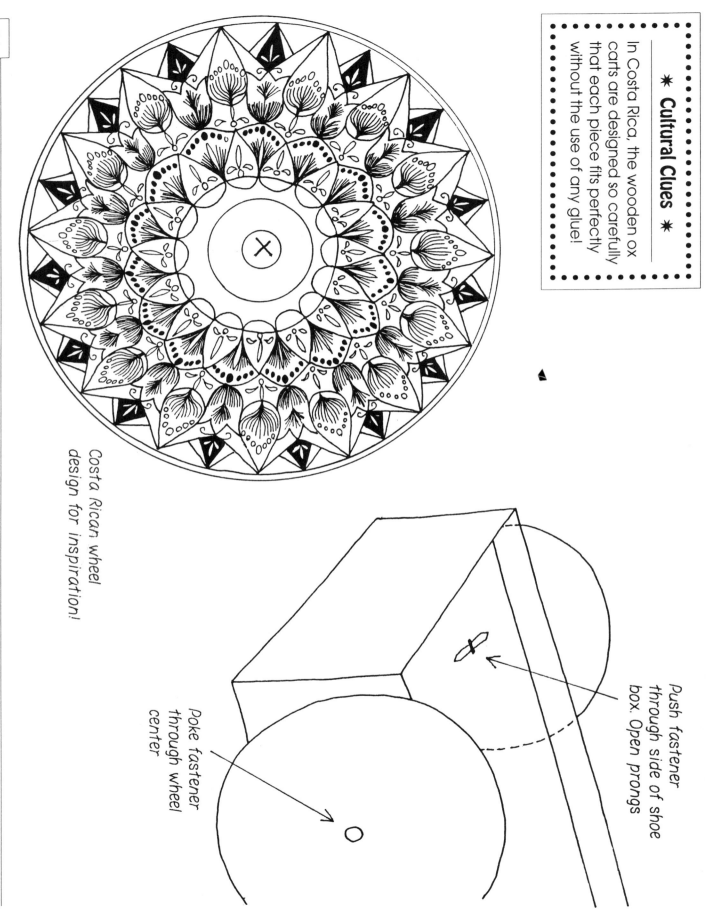

Costa Rican wheel design for inspiration!

Push fastener through side of shoe box. Open prongs

Poke fastener through wheel center

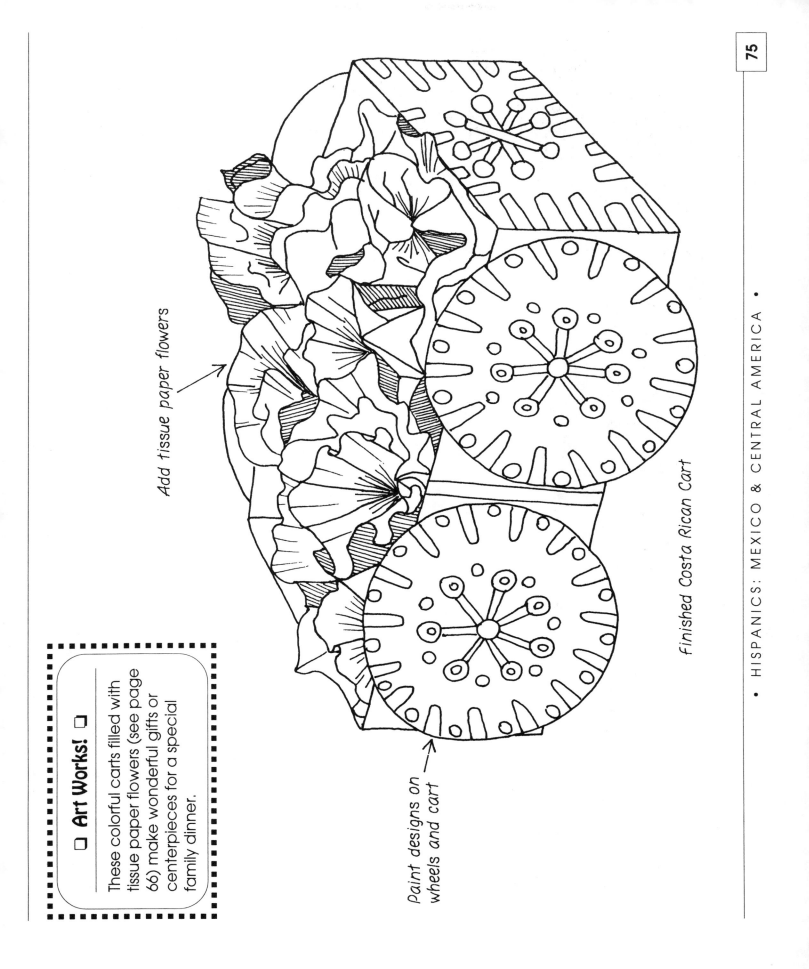

□ **Art Works!** □

These colorful carts filled with tissue paper flowers (see page 66) make wonderful gifts or centerpieces for a special family dinner.

Add tissue paper flowers

Paint designs on wheels and cart

Finished Costa Rican Cart

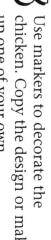

HONDURAN PAPER POLLO

*Pollo (POY-yo), or chicken, is an important part of cooking, as well as arts and crafts, in Honduras and other Central American countries. Shredded chicken can be found in a dish called enchiladas (en-CHEE-la-das). It is **muy delicioso**, or very delicious!*

◆ **MATERIALS** ◆

Scrap paper
(large enough to trace sample)

Yellow construction paper, about 7" x 10"

Markers, pencil, stapler, scissors

1. Trace the pattern of the chicken onto scrap paper and cut out.

2. Trace around the pattern onto the construction paper and cut out.

3. Use markers to decorate the chicken. Copy the design or make up one of your own.

4. Bend the ends around toward the back, overlap the ends, and staple closed.

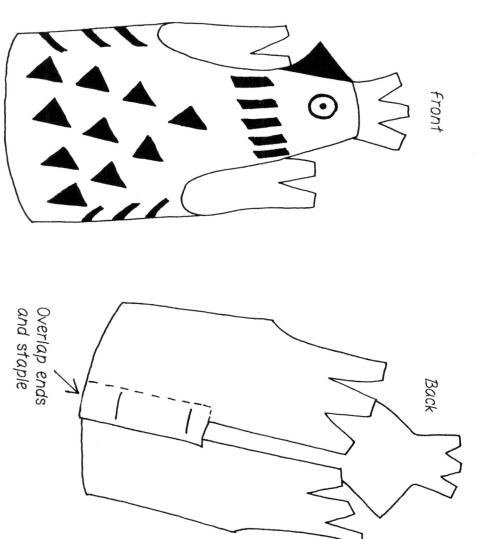

Front

Back

Overlap ends
and staple

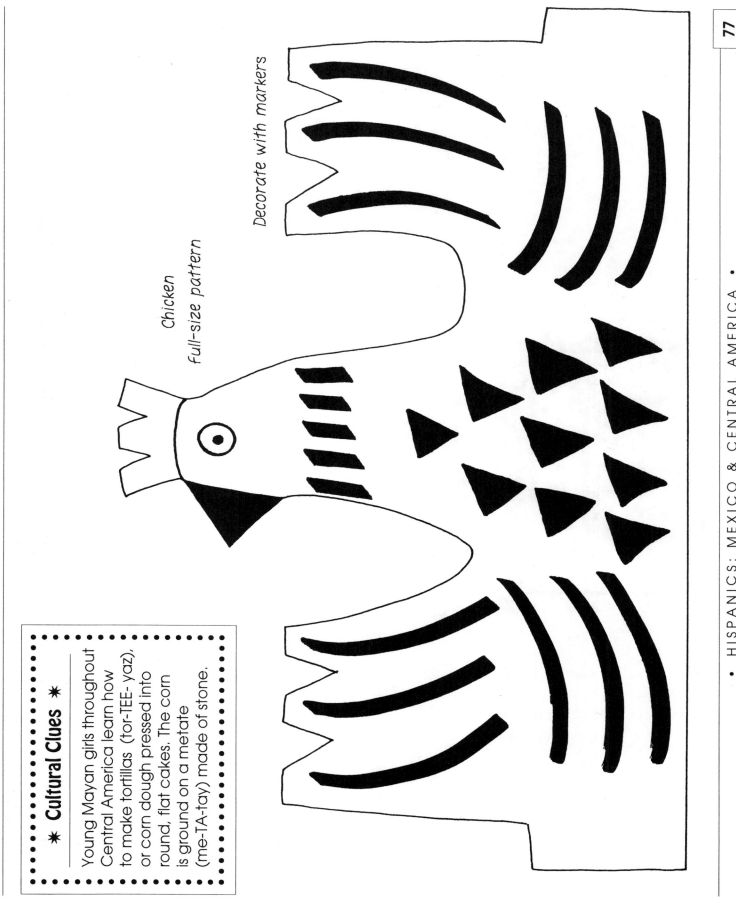

Decorate with markers

Chicken
full-size pattern

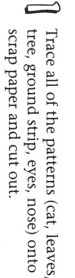

GUATEMALAN WILD CAT

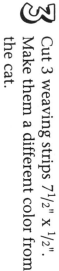

The jaguar and puma are two very ferocious wild cats that live in the Guatemalan forests and lowlands. The "wild" cat here is made of felt. The original popular design is an embroidery (hand-sewn on fabric) of a black and blue checkered tiger with her baby tiger, on a red background.

1. Trace all of the patterns (cat, leaves, tree, ground strip, eyes, nose) onto scrap paper and cut out.

2. Trace the patterns onto different colors of felt, using white pencil or chalk. Cut out all the shapes. Save one large piece of felt for backing.

3. Cut 3 weaving strips 7¹/₂" x ¹/₂". Make them a different color from the cat.

4. With your white pencil or chalk, draw 10 short lines on the side of the cat's body where the weaving will be. Poke and cut 10 slits along the body. Be careful to stop before you get to the edges.

◆ **M A T E R I A L S** ◆

Felt, 2 or 3 sheets, 7¹/₂" x 10", and some scraps in different colors

Yarn, white, 6 small pieces (for whiskers)

Scrap paper

White pencil or white chalk

Pencil, glue, scissors

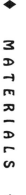

5. Take a weaving strip and weave it into the body of the cat as shown. Row 1 is *under*, over, under, over, until the end. Row 2 is *over*, under, over, under, until the end. Now repeat Row 1 and you are finished weaving.

6. Glue all the pieces onto the felt backing, as shown, or make up your own design. Glue on the yarn pieces for whiskers. Felt needs a lot of glue in order to stick. Lay a heavy object over the design to dry for several hours or overnight. Now, hang on the wall using tacks.

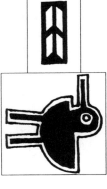

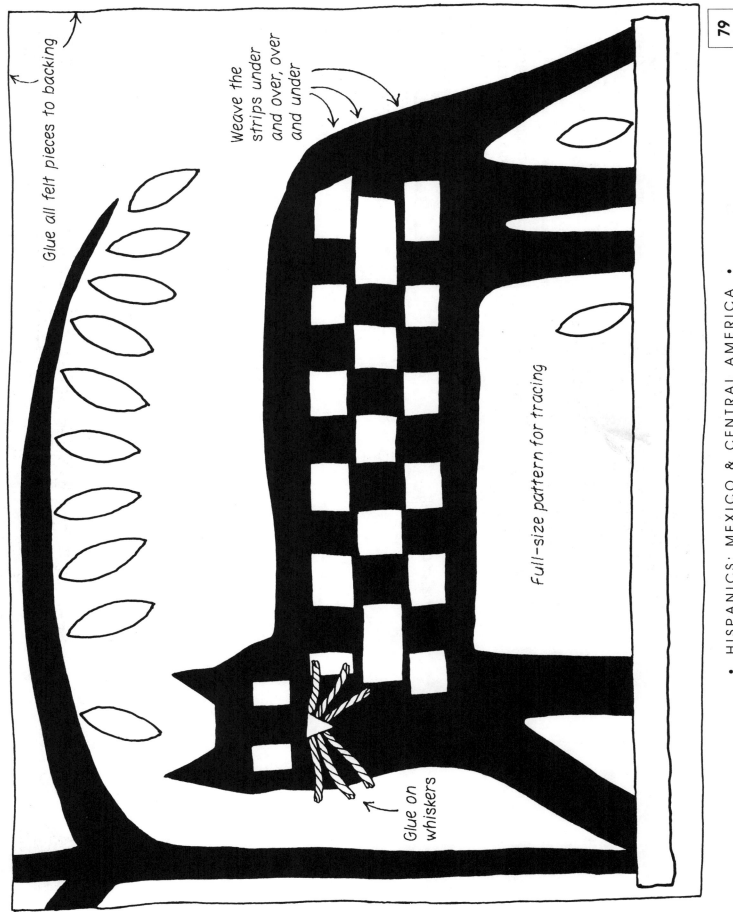

Glue all felt pieces to backing

Weave the strips under and over, over and under

Full-size pattern for tracing

Glue on whiskers

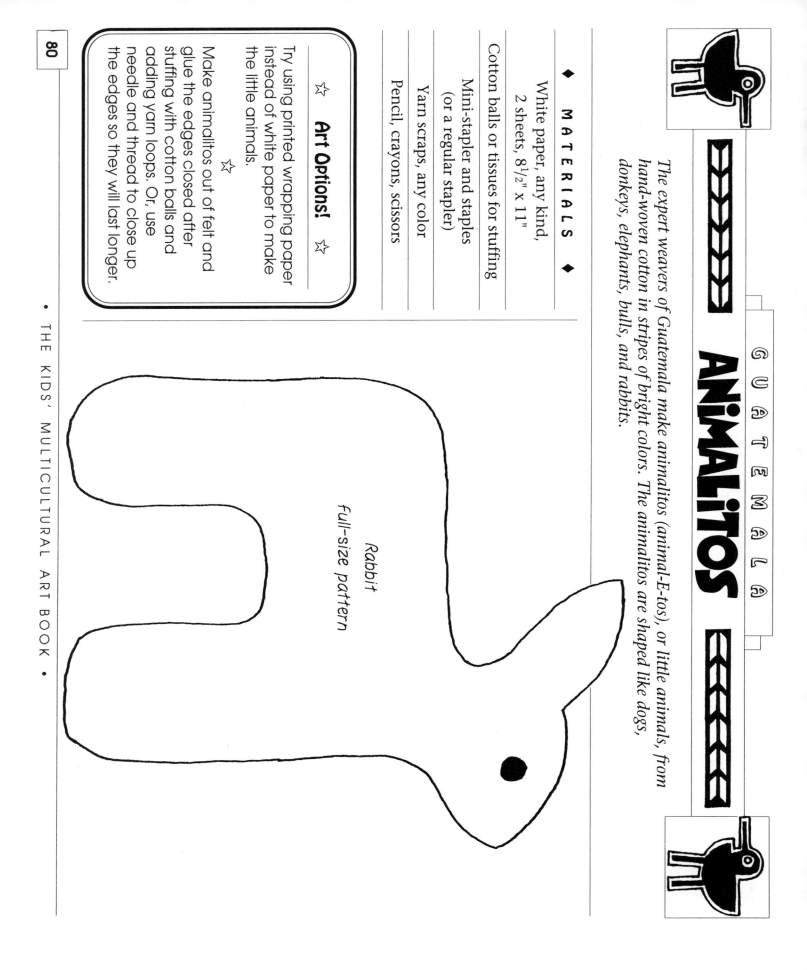

GUATEMALA

ANIMALITOS

The expert weavers of Guatemala make animalitos (animal-E-tos), or little animals, from hand-woven cotton in stripes of bright colors. The animalitos are shaped like dogs, donkeys, elephants, bulls, and rabbits.

◆ MATERIALS ◆

White paper, any kind,
2 sheets, 8½" x 11"

Cotton balls or tissues for stuffing

Mini-stapler and staples
(or a regular stapler)

Yarn scraps, any color

Pencil, crayons, scissors

☆ Art Options! ☆

Try using printed wrapping paper instead of white paper to make the little animals.

☆

Make animalitos out of felt and glue the edges closed after stuffing with cotton balls and adding yarn loops. Or, use needle and thread to close up the edges so they will last longer.

Rabbit
full-size pattern

1 Trace the full-size pattern (or draw your own) two times onto paper. Cut out. You will have two pieces just alike.

2 Place the two animal pieces on the table so their noses face each other. Use a colorful variety of crayons to add stripes or diagonals, making both animal pieces look alike. Add dark, round eyes to both pieces.

3 With the crayon side out, staple the two pieces together around the bottom half as shown.

4 At the opening, stuff the animal. Staple on loops of yarn for the tail and/or the mane, and a loop at the top of the head for hanging. Finish stapling and add a yarn bow around the neck.

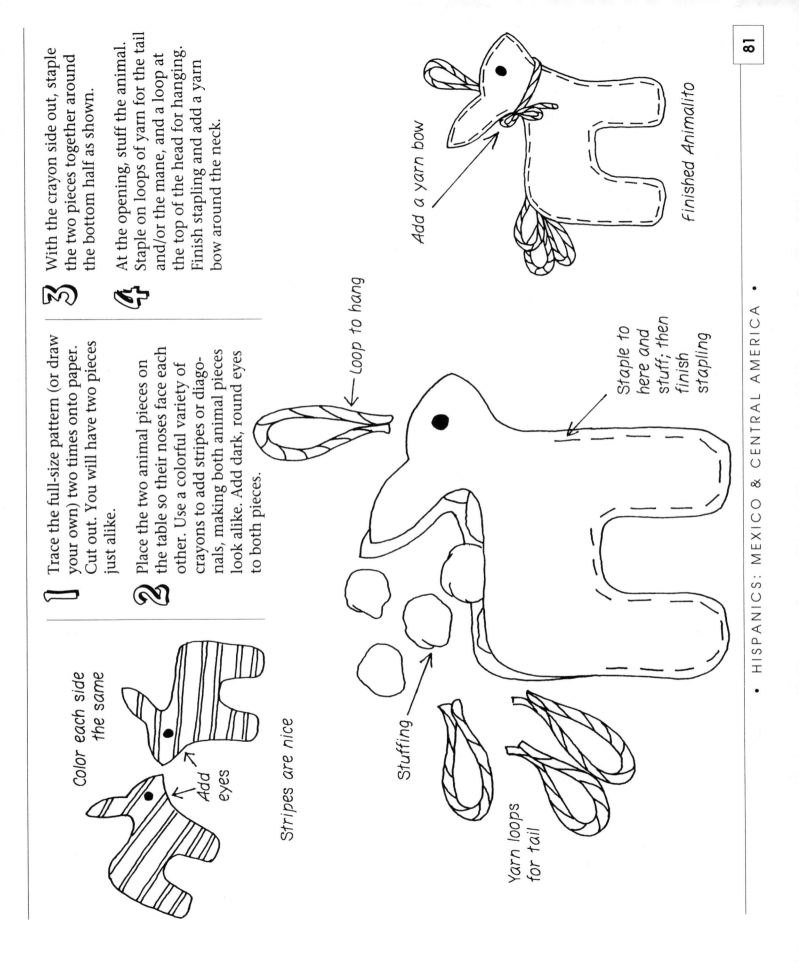

Color each side the same

Add eyes

Stripes are nice

Loop to hang

Staple to here and stuff; then finish stapling

Stuffing

Yarn loops for tail

Add a yarn bow

Finished Animalito

GUATEMALAN PLATE DESIGNS

These are four Guatemalan designs adapted from glazed pottery plates. The colors of the glazes (glasslike coating fired on the clay at high temperatures) are green, yellow, brown, and blue. Using white paper plates and some paint, you can create these wonderful designs to hang anywhere.

◆ MATERIALS ◆

Paper plates, 9" white

Tempera paint in small cups

Yarn to hang

Paintbrushes, pencil, hole punch

1 Sketch one of the designs onto a paper plate. It does not have to be exact. Or, make up a similar type of design.

2 Paint on the designs, using the colors any way you wish.

3 Punch a hole at the top and add a yarn loop to hang. Try all four designs and hang in a group on the wall, for added impact.

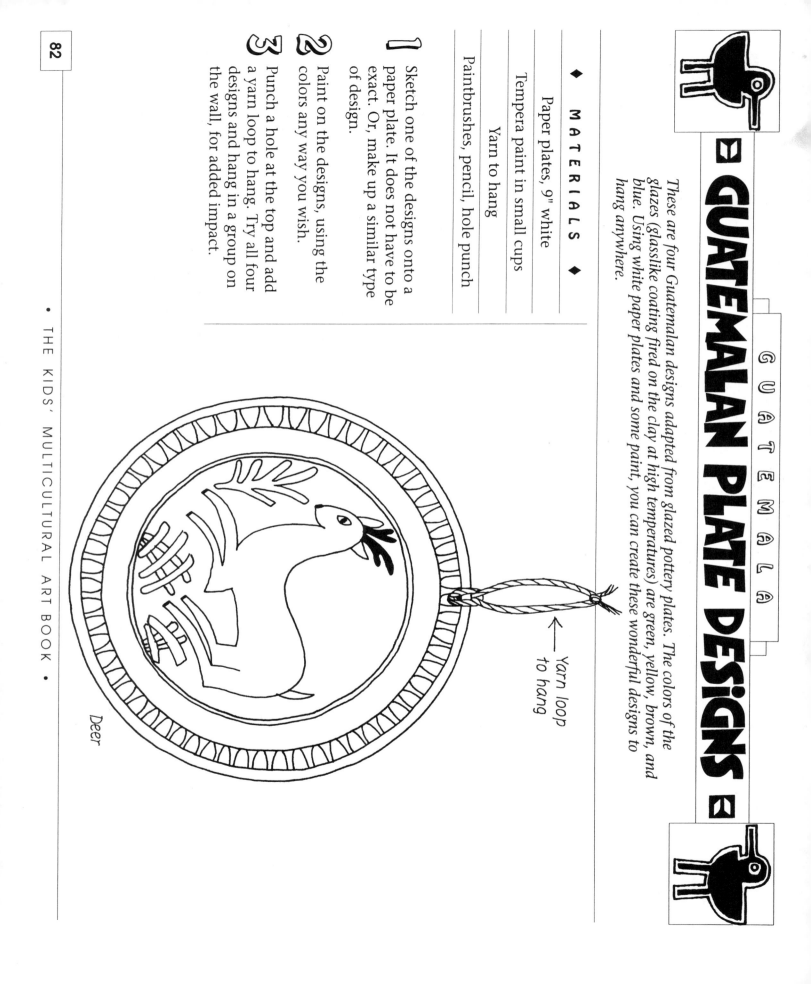

← Yarn loop to hang

Deer

Use one or all of these designs from Guatemala. (Does not have to be exact)

Sun

Flowers

Punch a hole

GREEN TOAD BANK

Clay banks are very popular throughout Mexico and Central America. In Guatemala, clay green toad banks are hand-painted with pretty flowers. Your green toad bank, made from papier-mache, can be painted with a Guatemalan design.

Paint toad green, then decorate

finished Green Toad Bank

◆ MATERIALS ◆

Papier-mache paste (see page 152 for recipe) in bowl

Newspaper strips

Round balloon, any color*

Cardboard, about 5" x 7"

Scrap white paper, 5" x 7"

Tempera paints, green and any other colors, in small cups

Acrylic gloss varnish in small cup

Paintbrushes, pencil, glue, scissors

1   Blow up the balloon and tie it closed.

2   Follow the instructions on page 152 for covering the entire balloon with papier-mache paste and newspaper strips. Let the first layer dry (overnight is best). Add a second and third layer of papier-mache, letting each layer dry completely.

*See warning, page 9.

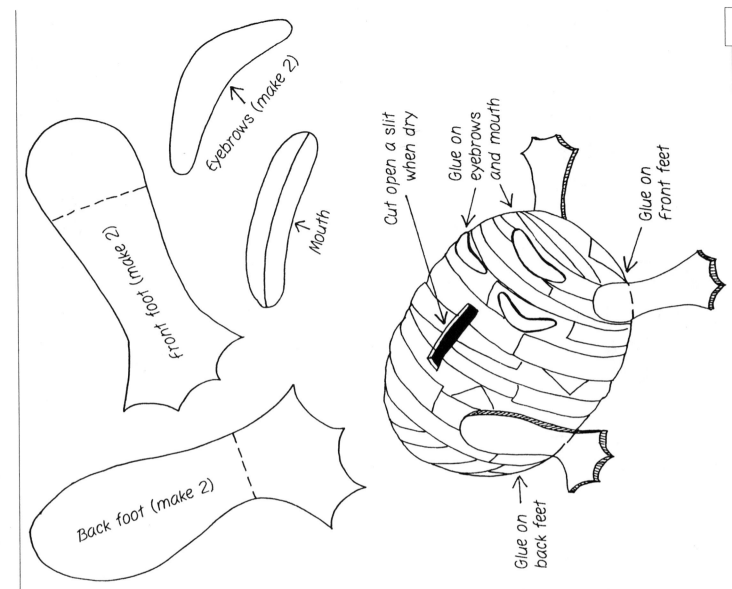

Front foot (make 2)

Eyebrows (make 2)

Mouth

Back foot (make 2)

Cut open a slit when dry

Glue on eyebrows and mouth

Glue on front feet

Glue on back feet

3 When dry, cut a slit about 2"–3" long and about ½" wide in the balloon as shown (the balloon will pop). Try to remove the piece of balloon by shaking lightly. Put all balloon pieces in the trash right away.

4 Trace the feet, the mouth, and the eyebrows onto scrap paper, and cut out. Trace patterns onto the cardboard and cut out. Fold the feet on the fold lines.

5 With the slit at the top, glue the mouth, eyebrows, and front and back feet onto the bank as shown. Let dry completely. Your bank should now look like a toad.

6 Using a wide brush, paint the whole bank green. Cover the mouth, eyebrows, and the feet. Paint the top part first and allow to dry. Then, flip the toad over and paint the bottom. Let this dry.

7 Use dark-colored paint on the eyebrows and the eyes. Paint flowers and other designs around the body with other colors. Let it dry.

8 Apply the varnish to the top of the toad bank with a large, clean brush, letting top dry before varnishing bottom.

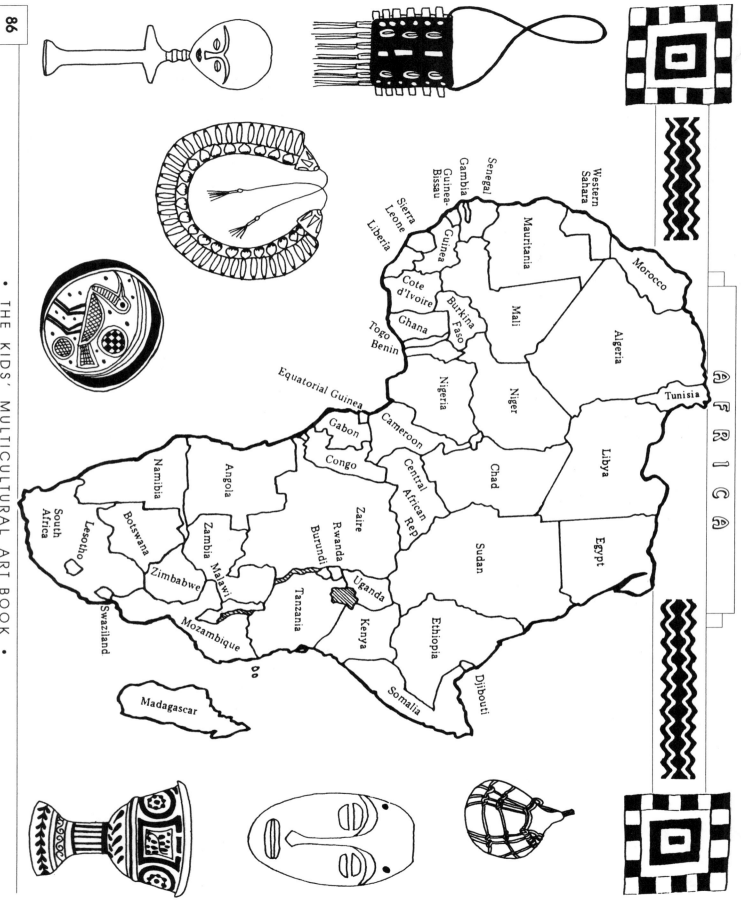

AFRICA

Western
Sahara

Mauritania

Morocco

Senegal
Gambia
Guinea-
Bissau
Guinea

Sierra
Leone

Liberia

Mali

Algeria

Cote
d'Ivoire

Burkina
Faso

Ghana

Togo
Benin

Nigeria

Niger

Tunisia

Equatorial Guinea

Cameroon

Libya

Gabon

Congo

Central
African
Rep

Chad

Namibia

Angola

Zaire

Egypt

Rwanda
Burundi

Botswana

Zambia

Sudan

South
Africa

Lesotho

Zimbabwe

Malawi

Uganda

Tanzania

Kenya

Ethiopia

Swaziland

Mozambique

Somalia

Djibouti

Madagascar

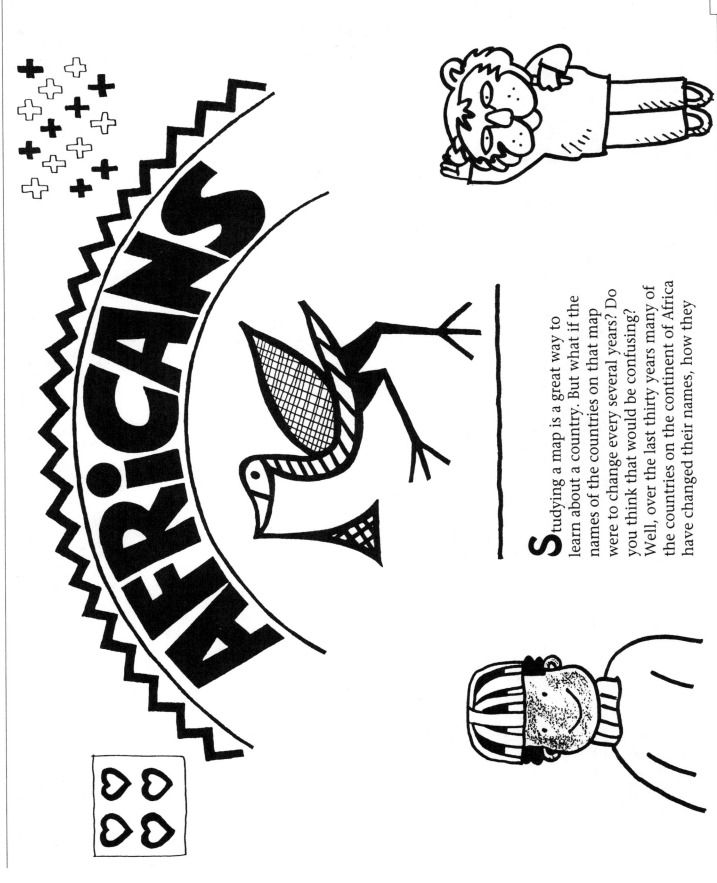

AFRICANS

Studying a map is a great way to learn about a country. But what if the names of the countries on that map were to change every several years? Do you think that would be confusing? Well, over the last thirty years many of the countries on the continent of Africa have changed their names, how they

are governed, and their flags in honor of their newfound independence from the European countries that once governed them. The map included in this book has the latest names of the fifty countries in Africa including Madagascar, a large island off the east coast.

But Africa's cultural traditions go back thousands of years and have richly influenced the world over, especially the Caribbean, the United States, Spain, France, the Mediterranean, the Middle East, and many Asian countries. During 1500-1800, about 10 million African men, women, and children were sent to the Americas as part of the Atlantic slave trade, bringing with them their

strong heritage which continues to enrich the Americas today.

For centuries, African sculptors, using shapes, patterns, and textures, have created figures and animals that seem to spring to life! Pouches with traditional designs dyed into the leather are handcrafted with care. These skills and many more are passed from parents to their children.

Masks and face-painting are an important part of African religious and ceremonial life. Wood, ivory, bone, and metal are used to make masks, and some even have hair, feathers, and beads attached to them. The men and

women who wear masks are usually members of a special club or society. The place where the masks are made and where the ceremonial dancers get dressed is kept secret, but when they perform to the rhythm of the drums, everyone is invited. By creating your own African animal mask, you can make a lion or camel come alive with the simplest of materials.

You'll get a chance to experience some of the magic found in Africa's diverse and rich heritage as you create your own African-inspired art and craft projects. No matter what you choose to make, you're sure to discover something exciting about Africa and the people who call this beautiful land "home."

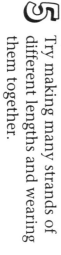
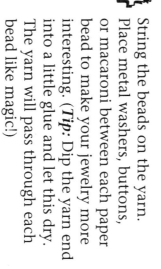
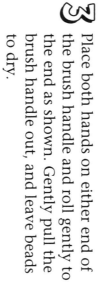

EGYPTIAN PAPER BEADS

The people of Egypt have been making beads since the time when the great pyramids were built, 5,000 years ago! They wore wide collars of beads made from gems, glass, or ceramics for decoration. Today, African tribal groups wear many strings of beads and also embroider, or sew, beads onto their bags, pouches, and clothing.

◆ **MATERIALS** ◆

Brightly colored magazine pages

Yarn, long enough to make a necklace or a bracelet

Metal washers (available at hardware stores), buttons, or macaroni

Paintbrush handle, glue, scissors

1. Cut magazine pages into 1" strips, and spread glue all over each strip.

2. Place the brush handle on one end of the paper strip. Fold the end of the strip over the handle and press down. The glue will hold it down.

3. Place both hands on either end of the brush handle and roll gently to the end as shown. Gently pull the brush handle out, and leave beads to dry.

4. String the beads on the yarn. Place metal washers, buttons, or macaroni between each paper bead to make your jewelry more interesting. (*Tip:* Dip the yarn end into a little glue and let this dry. The yarn will pass through each bead like magic!)

5. Try making many strands of different lengths and wearing them together.

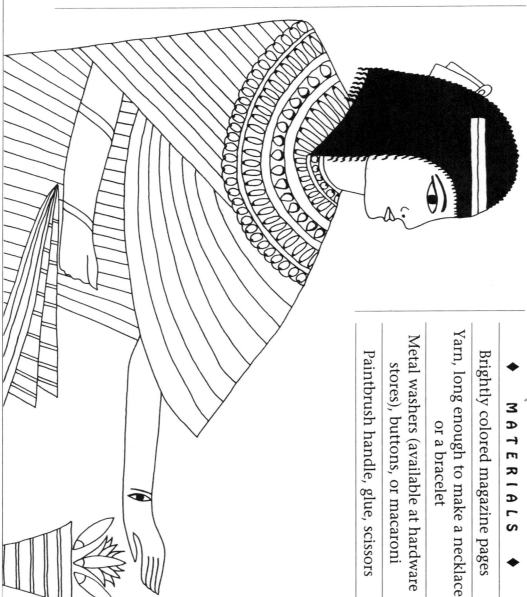

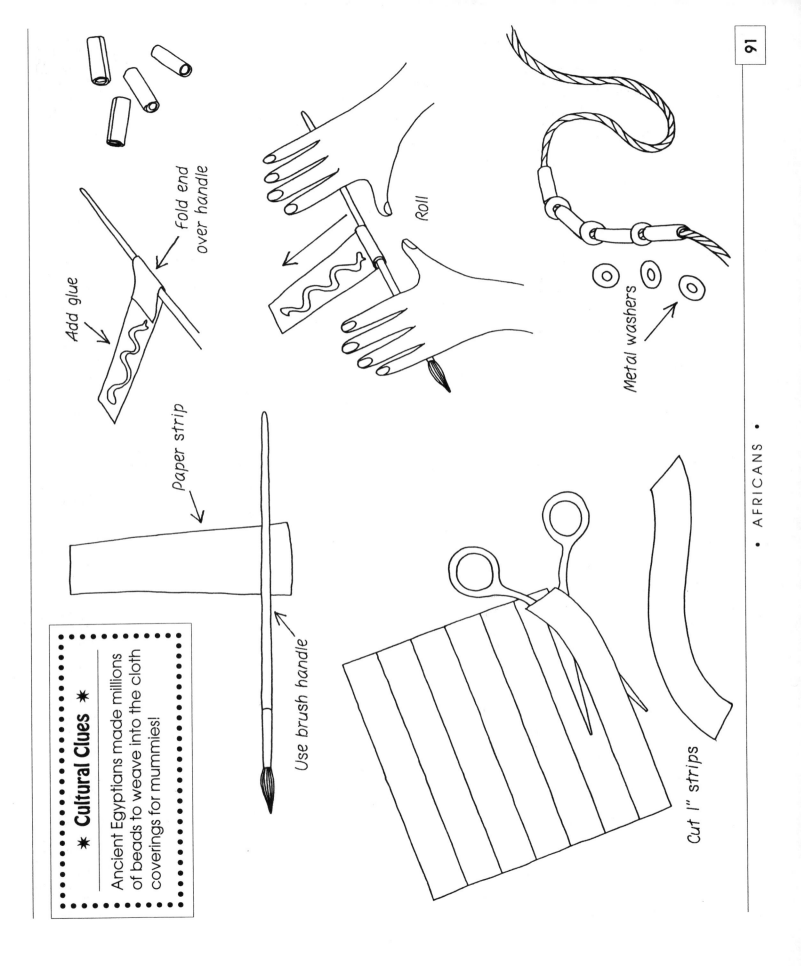

Add glue

Fold end
over handle

Paper strip

Roll

Metal washers

Use brush handle

Cut 1" strips

AFRICAN ADORNMENT

WODAABE MIRROR POUCH

The Wodaabe (woe-DA-bee) people of Niger wear leather mirror pouches decorated with cowrie shells, beads, copper, and more, around their necks. Other Africans use found objects like large safety pins and even pieces of zippers in their arts and crafts.

1. Fold the poster board in half. Open it and draw a 2" x 3" box in the middle of the top half, as shown. Starting on left side of the box, cut up and around on three sides (leave the bottom edge attached) to form a flap.

2. Push the flap through to the other side and glue or tape the aluminum foil to cover the inside opening.

3. Fold the poster board closed. With edges closed, punch holes through both layers around three sides, but not the folded edge. To sew together, pull gimp or string through top hole, leaving a fairly long tail. Feed in and out all the way around to the top of the other side. Even the ends around the back of your neck, and knot them.

4. Glue on decorative items. The Wodaabe place decorations in rows on their pouches.

5. To add fringe, tie or glue long pieces of gimp, string, or strips of gold foil along the bottom edge. Hang the pouch around your neck.

◆ M A T E R I A L S ◆

Poster board or tagboard, any dark color, 5" x 10"

Gimp or string, any color, 3' long

Aluminum foil, 3" x 4"

Pencil, glue or tape, scissors, hole punch

For decoration: Beads, buttons, gold foil, small shells, safety pins, bits of colored paper

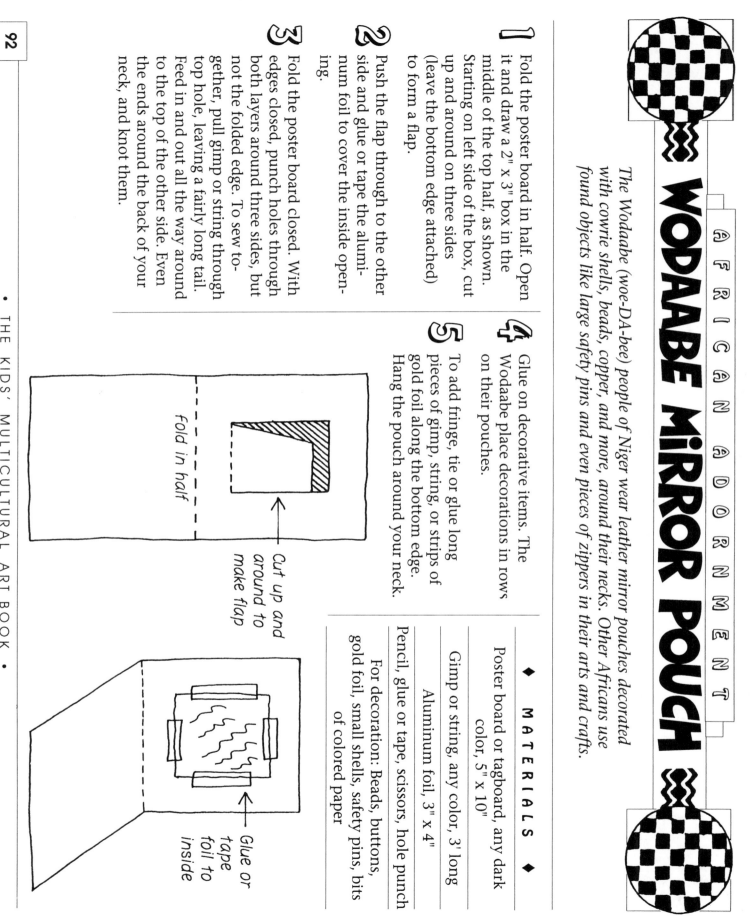

Fold in half

Cut up and around to make flap

Glue or tape foil to inside

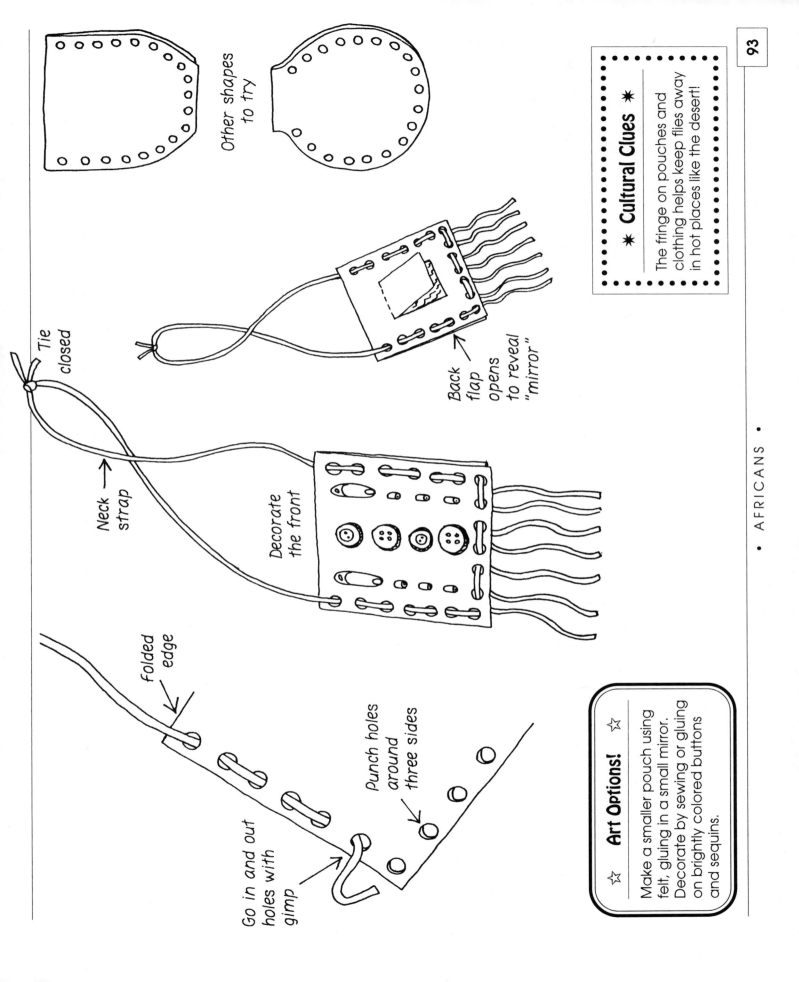

Other shapes
to try

Tie
closed

Neck
strap

Back
flap
opens
to reveal
"mirror"

Decorate
the front

Folded
edge

Go in and out
holes with
gimp

Punch holes
around
three sides

* AFRICANS *

☀ **Cultural Clues** ☀

The fringe on pouches and
clothing helps keep flies away
in hot places like the desert!

☆ **Art Options!** ☆

Make a smaller pouch using
felt, gluing in a small mirror.
Decorate by sewing or gluing
on brightly colored buttons
and sequins.

PAPER KUFi

To show pride in their heritage, young African-Americans and young Africans often wear a round hat called a kufi (KOO-fee). Some are made from kente (KEN-tay) cloth, a material made in Ghana. Making and wearing kufis is a great way to acknowledge the importance of Black History Month, celebrated in February in the United States.

◆ **MATERIALS** ◆

Dark-colored construction paper for headband (24" long x 2" wide)

6 strips of construction paper (12" long x 1" wide) as follows: 2 red, 2 yellow, 2 green, or any other colors you wish

Scissors, stapler

1 Fit the headband snugly around your head, and staple together.

2 Arrange the six strips of colored paper so they overlap to form a wheel as shown. Staple at the center.

3 To connect to headband, place one strip along the outside edge of the headband. Staple this down; then, do the same all the way around.

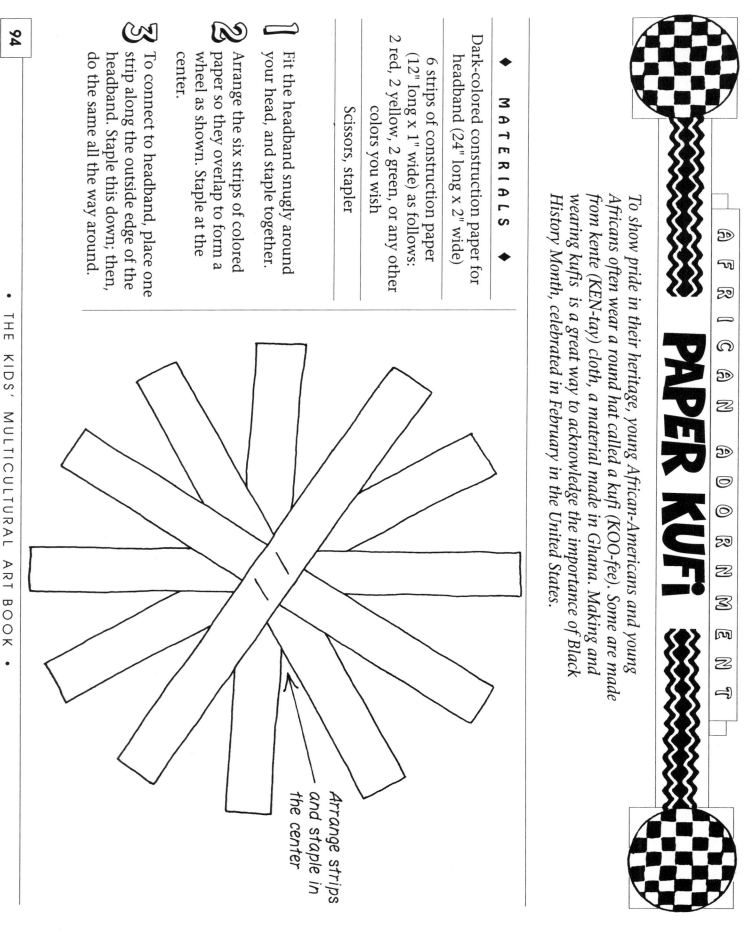

Arrange strips and staple in the center

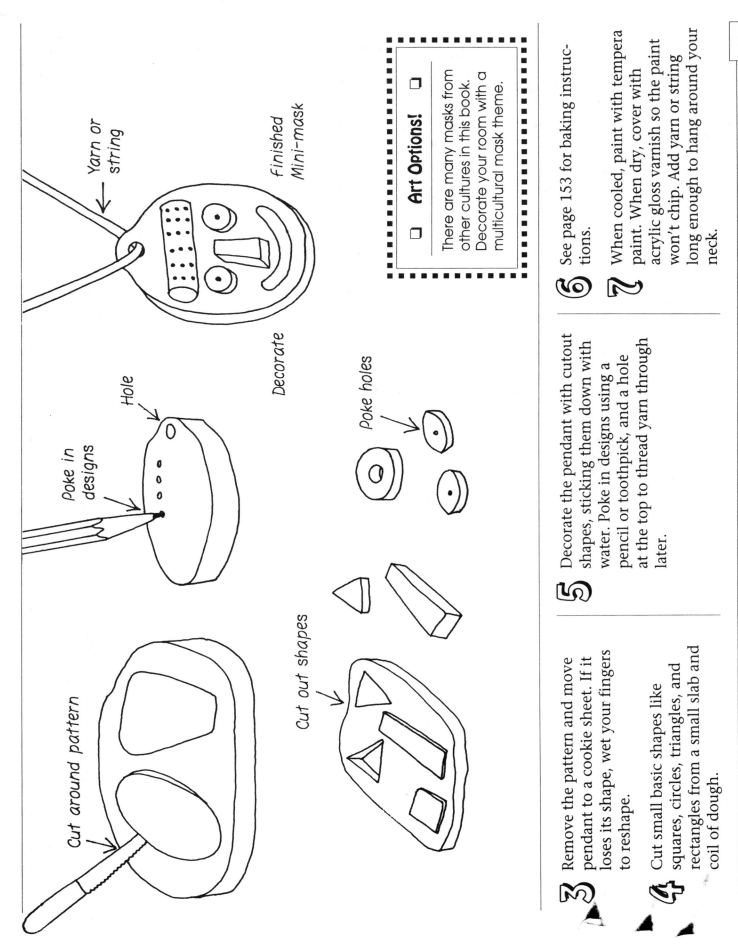

Yarn or string

Finished Mini-mask

Decorate

Hole

Poke in designs

Poke holes

Cut around pattern

Cut out shapes

Art Options! ☐ ☐

There are many masks from other cultures in this book. Decorate your room with a multicultural mask theme.

3 Remove the pattern and move pendant to a cookie sheet. If it loses its shape, wet your fingers to reshape.

4 Cut small basic shapes like squares, circles, triangles, and rectangles from a small slab and coil of dough.

5 Decorate the pendant with cutout shapes, sticking them down with water. Poke in designs using a pencil or toothpick, and a hole at the top to thread yarn through later.

6 See page 153 for baking instructions.

7 When cooled, paint with tempera paint. When dry, cover with acrylic gloss varnish so the paint won't chip. Add yarn or string long enough to hang around your neck.

AFRICAN MASKS

AniMAL NOSE MASKS

African mask carvers sometimes make masks that look like animals, such as the lion. Here's a simple lion mask that uses your nose at the center.

◆ MATERIALS ◆

Scrap paper

Light-colored poster board, 6" x 9"

Wooden tongue depressor
or Popsicle stick

Markers, pencil, glue, scissors

1. Trace the outline of the lion's face, including its nose and eyes onto scrap paper. Cut out the mask pattern, cutting out the eye holes and nose shape, too.

2. Trace the pattern onto the poster board, and cut out, including the nose and eye holes.

3. Color your mask, using your imagination.

4. Glue the wooden tongue depressor to the inside, along one bottom side to make a handle. Place the nose mask over your nose and make growling noises. Now you are something else!

✳ Cultural Clues ✳

The cheetah and the leopard are two other wild cats from Africa.

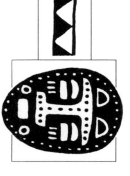

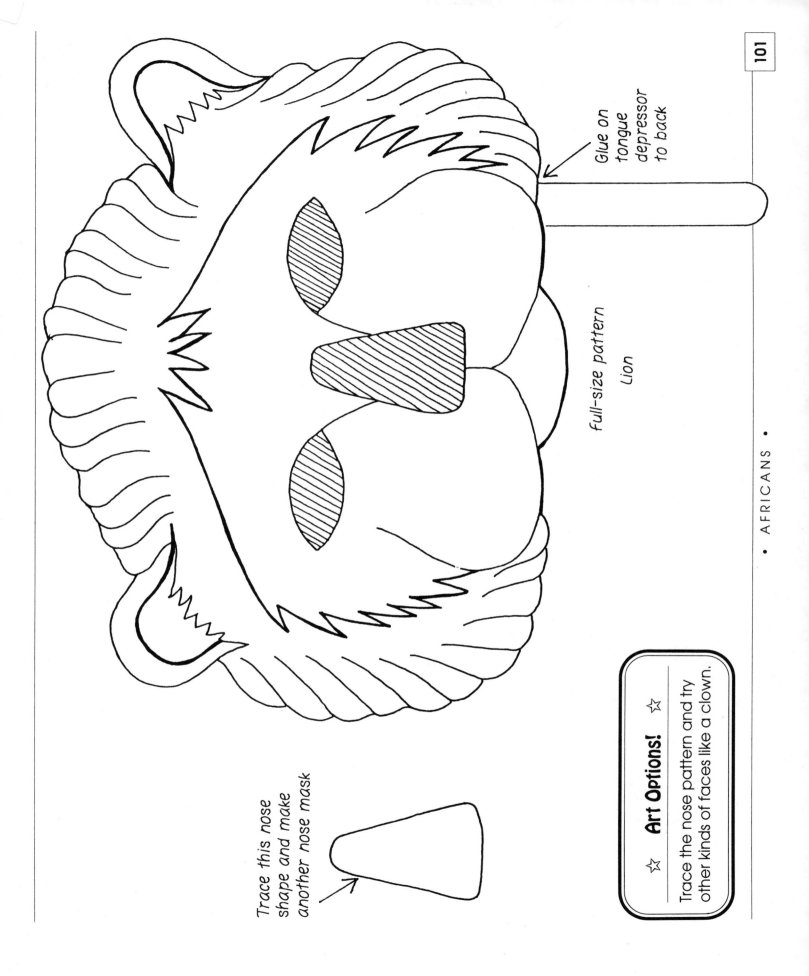

Trace this nose
shape and make
another nose mask

Glue on
tongue
depressor
to back

Full-size pattern
Lion

☆ **Art Options!** ☆

Trace the nose pattern and try
other kinds of faces like a clown.

PAPIER-MACHE CALABASH

Calabashes are bowls made from gourds that are cut and dried. What makes the calabashes so wonderful are the designs that the Africans paint, scratch, or burn on them. By using inexpensive papier-mache, your calabash will last for years.

◆ MATERIALS ◆

Papier-mache paste (see page 152 for recipe) in bowl
Newspaper strips
Bowl to use as mold (a plastic margarine tub works well)
Tempera paints, any colors including black, in cups
Acrylic gloss varnish
Paintbrush, scissors

1 Turn the plastic bowl over. Follow the instructions on page 152 to completely cover the bowl with papier-mache paste and newspaper strips. Dry overnight.

2 Add a second and third layer of papier-mache. Let each layer dry completely.

3 Separate the papier-mache bowl from the plastic bowl. Trim the edge neatly.

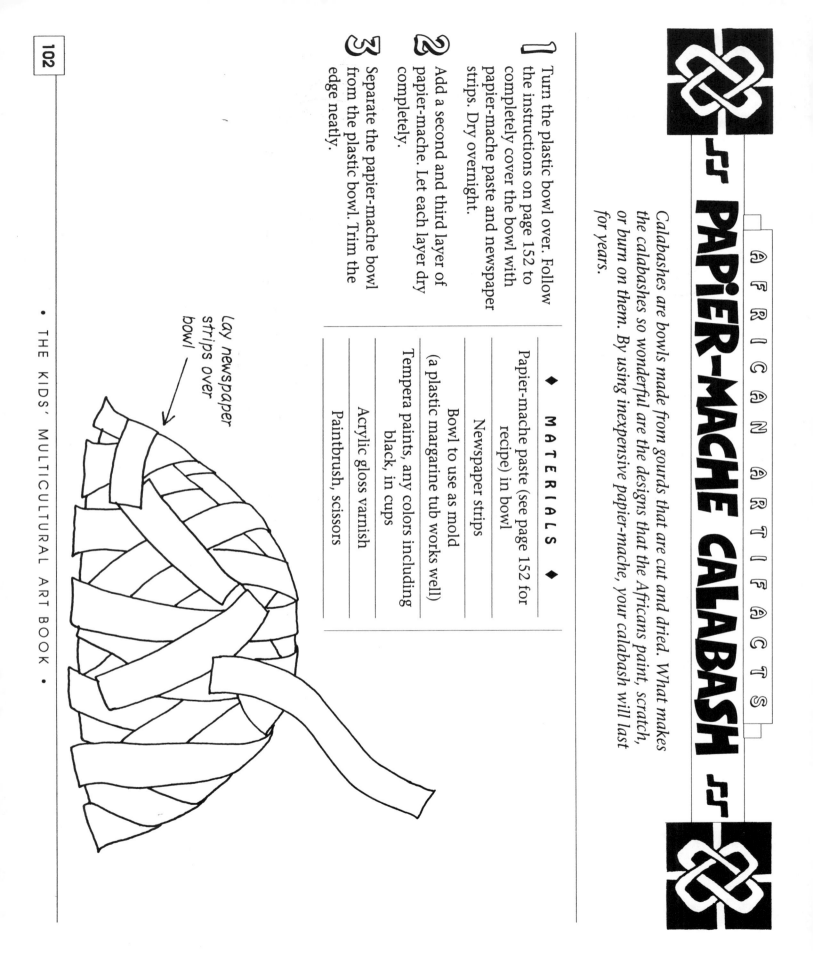

Lay newspaper strips over bowl

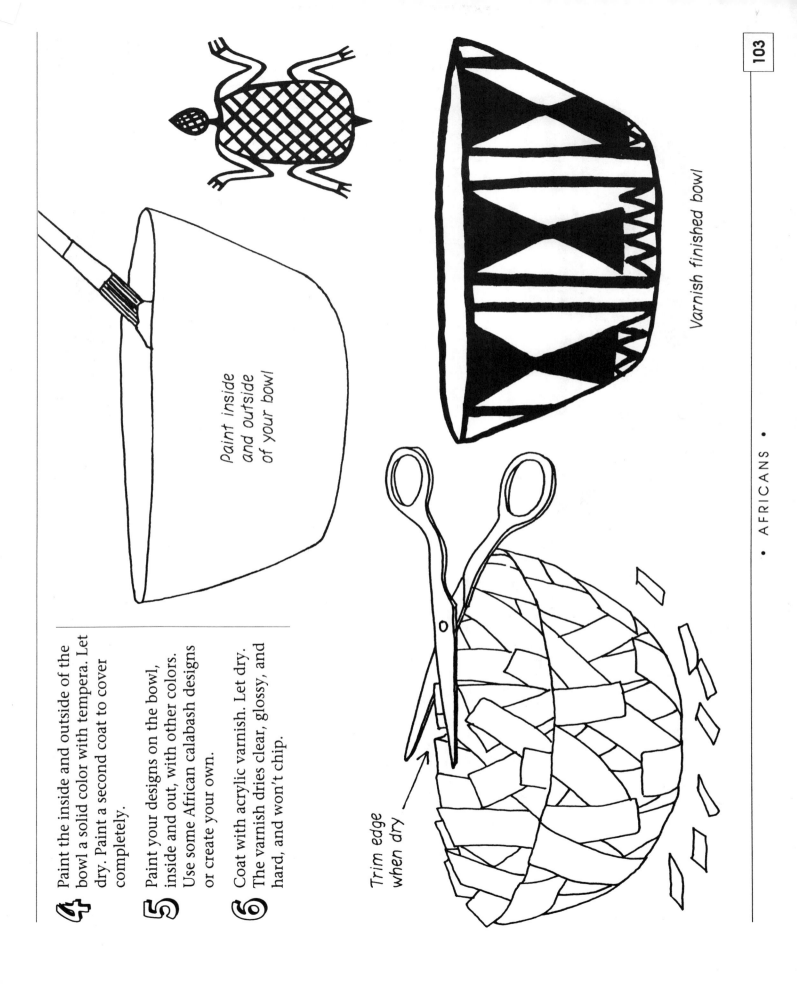

4 Paint the inside and outside of the bowl a solid color with tempera. Let dry. Paint a second coat to cover completely.

5 Paint your designs on the bowl, inside and out, with other colors. Use some African calabash designs or create your own.

6 Coat with acrylic varnish. Let dry. The varnish dries clear, glossy, and hard, and won't chip.

Paint inside and outside of your bowl

Varnish finished bowl

Trim edge when dry

Paint inside of bowl

These are African calabash designs.
Use these or make up your
own designs

☐ **Art Works!** ☐

Use your calabash to hold
a bouquet of dried flowers,
paper clips, or a special
collection of your own.

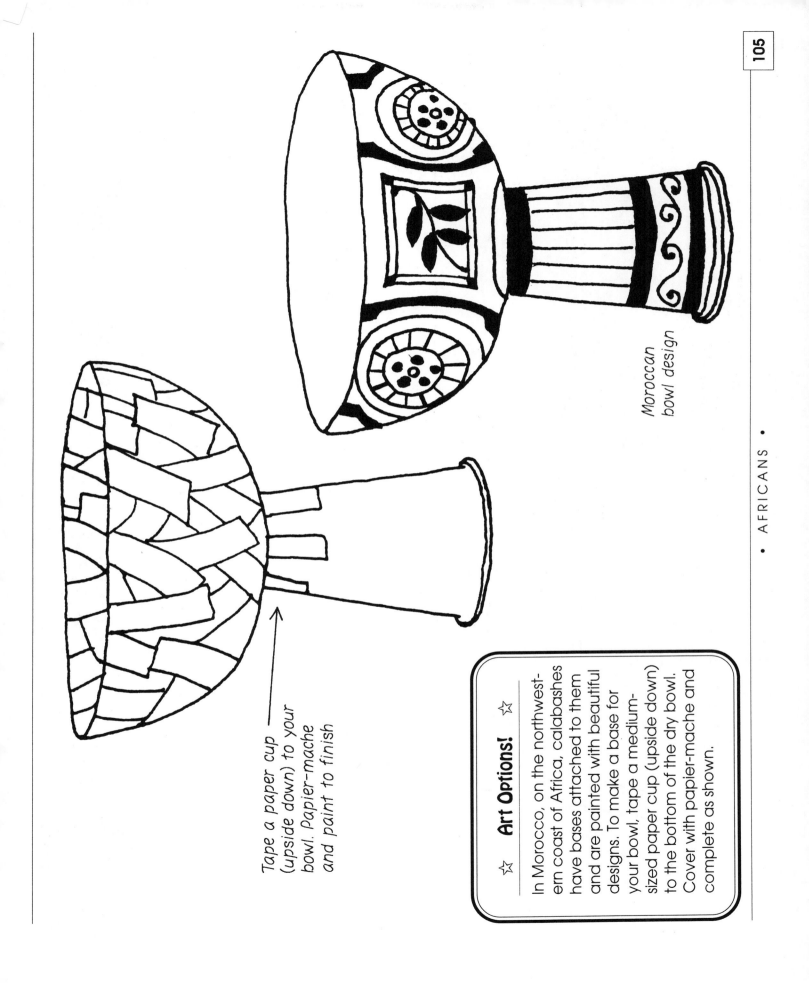

Tape a paper cup (upside down) to your bowl. Papier-mache and paint to finish

Moroccan bowl design

☆ **Art Options!** ☆

In Morocco, on the northwestern coast of Africa, calabashes have bases attached to them and are painted with beautiful designs. To make a base for your bowl, tape a medium-sized paper cup (upside down) to the bottom of the dry bowl. Cover with papier-mache and complete as shown.

AKUA-BA DOLL

The Asante (a-SAN-tay) people of Ghana make a wooden doll called an akua-ba (a-KWA-ba) that has a very large, round head, short, outstretched arms, and a thin body. The doll, tucked into a skirt at the waist, is carried by girls who hope to have children in the future and by women who hope their children will be healthy and beautiful.

1   Trace all of the patterns onto scrap paper, and cut out. Tape the head and body patterns together at the neck by overlapping at the dotted lines.

2   Tape the patterns to the cardboard and trace. Do not forget the slot.

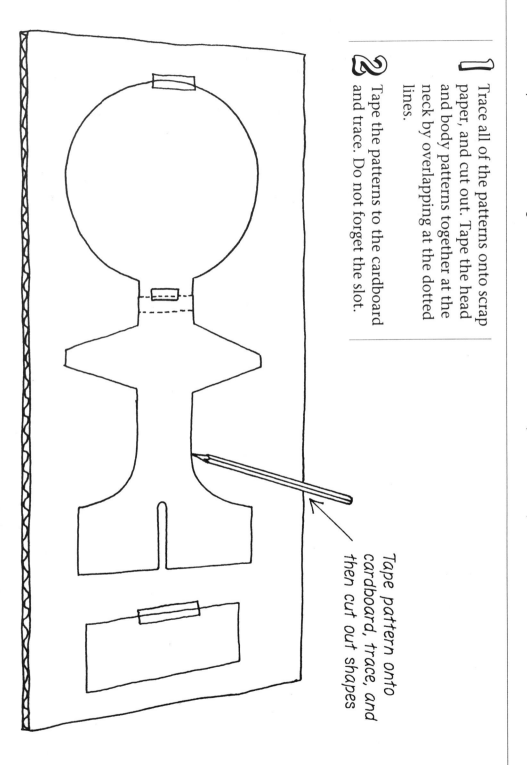

Tape pattern onto cardboard, trace, and then cut out shapes

◆ M A T E R I A L S ◆

Cardboard, about 8" x 18"

Scrap paper, about 8½" x 11"

Yarn, any color, about 3'

Tempera paint, brown and black, or dark color

Bowl

Paintbrushes, glue, tape, scissors

Mat knife or heavy duty scissors to be used by a grown-up only

3 Ask an older helper to cut pieces out with a mat knife or heavy duty scissors. (Remember to place a cutting board underneath to protect the table top.)

4 Squeeze out glue to form the facial features and the neck as shown. Then press the yarn down in it. Use one long piece of yarn, or cut it up into pieces. Let dry.

Press down yarn

Squeeze out glue

• A F R I C A N S •

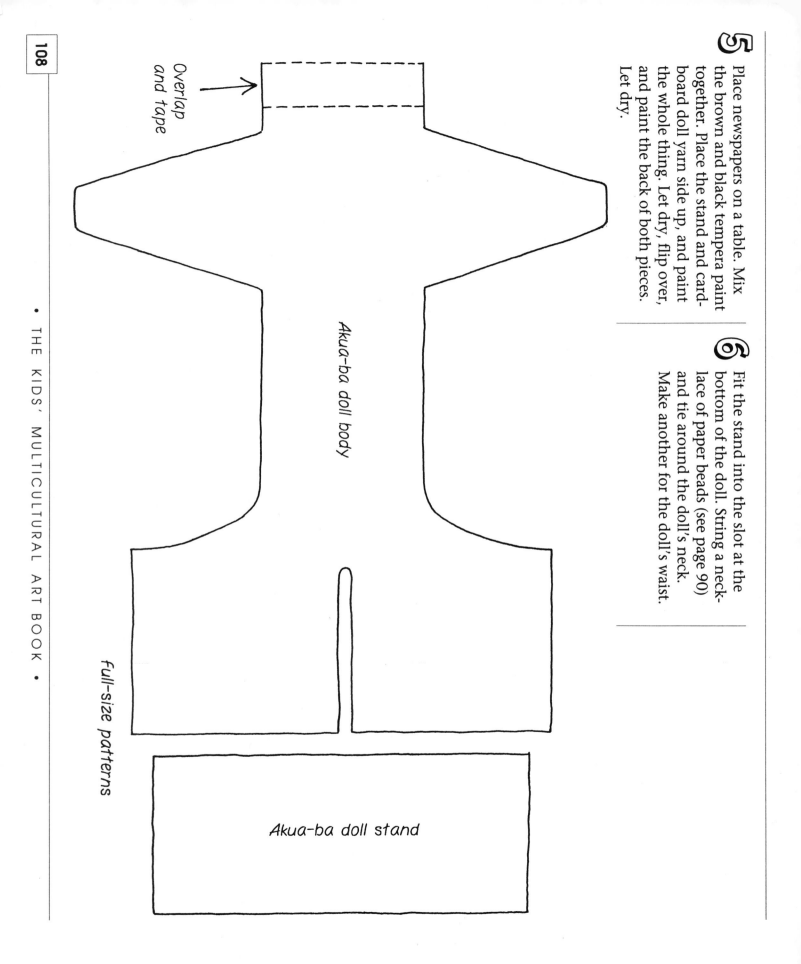

5 Place newspapers on a table. Mix the brown and black tempera paint together. Place the stand and cardboard doll yarn side up, and paint the whole thing. Let dry, flip over, and paint the back of both pieces. Let dry.

6 Fit the stand into the slot at the bottom of the doll. String a necklace of paper beads (see page 90) and tie around the doll's neck. Make another for the doll's waist.

Overlap and tape

Akua-ba doll body

Full-size patterns

Akua-ba doll stand

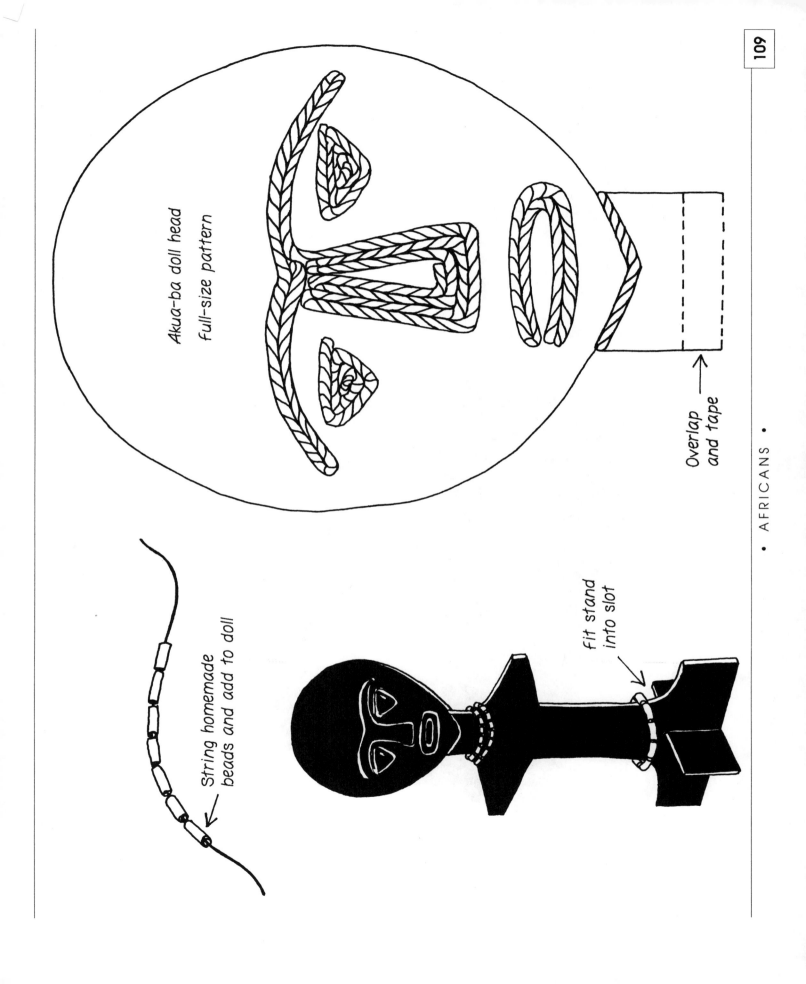

Akua-ba doll head
full-size pattern

Overlap and tape

String homemade beads and add to doll

fit stand into slot

KENTE PAPER WEAVING

Once made only for kings, kente (KEN-tay) cloth is still made by the Asante (a-SAN-tay) people of Ghana. The finely woven strips, made of rayon or silk, are sewn together, rolled up, and taken to market. This paper weaving uses colors similar to those found in kente cloth. It is very simple to make and looks great hanging on the wall.

◆ MATERIALS ◆

Black, or dark-colored construction paper, 12" x 18"

12 strips of construction paper, 12" x 1", as follows: 3 red, 3 yellow, 6 green

Wooden dowel (¹/₄"), 16" long

Yarn, any color, 20" long

1   Fold the black construction paper in half. Cut 1"-wide slits starting at the folded edge and cutting up. Stop 2" from the top.

2   Open up the black paper. Fold about 1" of the top edge toward the back. Glue the edge to the back, leaving a space for the dowel to pass through.

3   At the bottom edge, cut a fringe about 1¹/₂" in length.

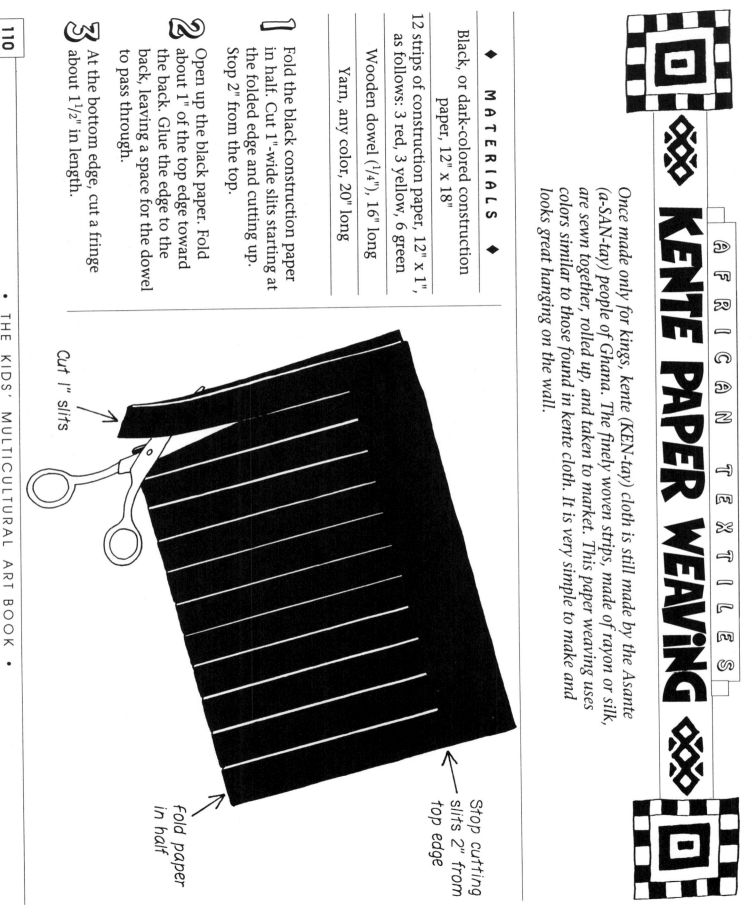

Cut 1" slits

Stop cutting slits 2" from top edge

fold paper in half

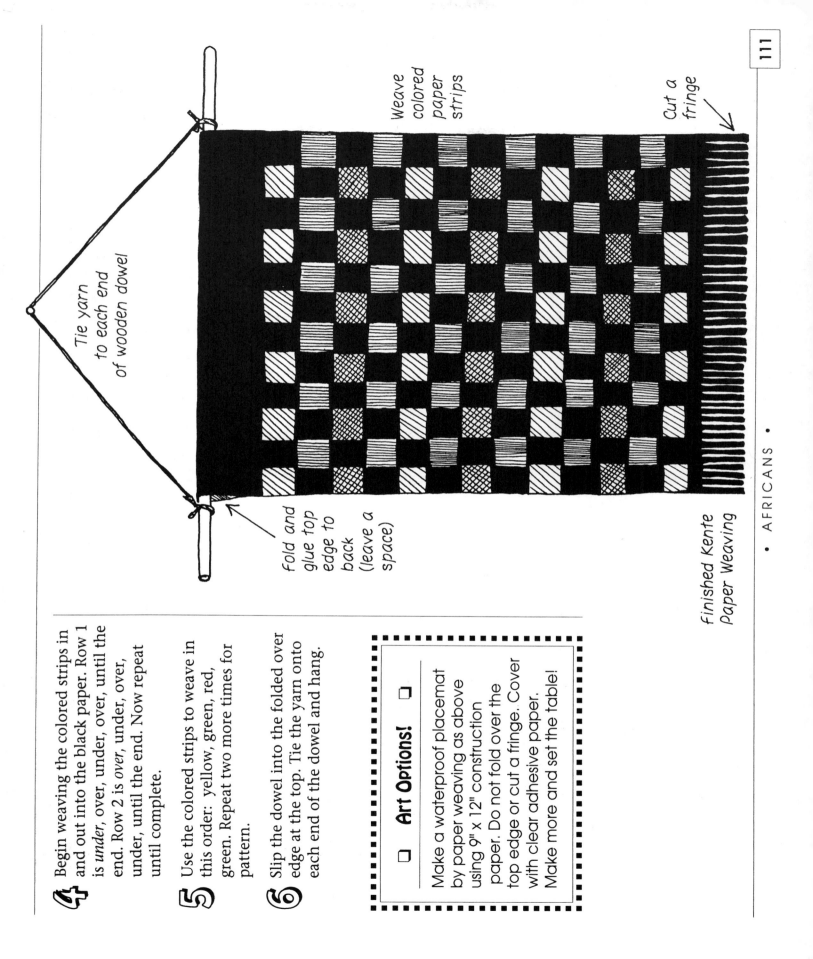

Tie yarn to each end of wooden dowel

Weave colored paper strips

Cut a fringe

Fold and glue top edge to back (leave a space)

Finished Kente Paper Weaving

4 Begin weaving the colored strips in and out into the black paper. Row 1 is *under*, over, under, over, until the end. Row 2 is *over*, under, over, under, until the end. Now repeat until complete.

5 Use the colored strips to weave in this order: yellow, green, red, green. Repeat two more times for pattern.

6 Slip the dowel into the folded over edge at the top. Tie the yarn onto each end of the dowel and hang.

☐ **Art Options!** ☐

Make a waterproof placemat by paper weaving as above using 9" x 12" construction paper. Do not fold over the top edge or cut a fringe. Cover with clear adhesive paper. Make more and set the table!

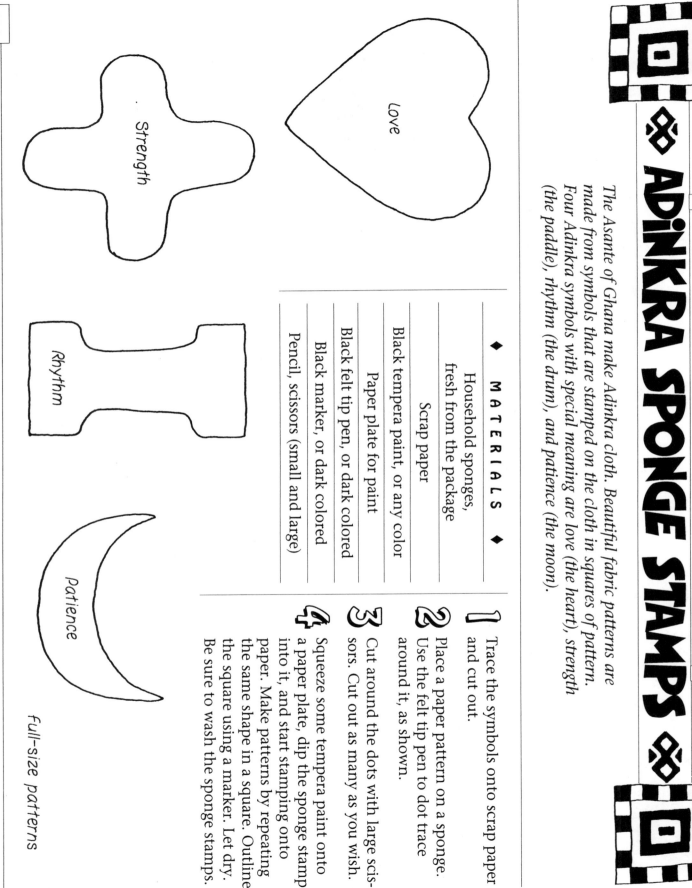

ADINKRA SPONGE STAMPS

The Asante of Ghana make Adinkra cloth. Beautiful fabric patterns are made from symbols that are stamped on the cloth in squares of pattern. Four Adinkra symbols with special meaning are love (the heart), strength (the paddle), rhythm (the drum), and patience (the moon).

◆ **M A T E R I A L S** ◆

Household sponges, fresh from the package

Scrap paper

Black tempera paint, or any color

Paper plate for paint

Black felt tip pen, or dark colored

Black marker, or dark colored

Pencil, scissors (small and large)

1. Trace the symbols onto scrap paper and cut out.

2. Place a paper pattern on a sponge. Use the felt tip pen to dot trace around it, as shown.

3. Cut around the dots with large scissors. Cut out as many as you wish.

4. Squeeze some tempera paint onto a paper plate, dip the sponge stamp into it, and start stamping onto paper. Make patterns by repeating the same shape in a square. Outline the square using a marker. Let dry. Be sure to wash the sponge stamps.

Love

Strength

Rhythm

Patience

Full-size patterns

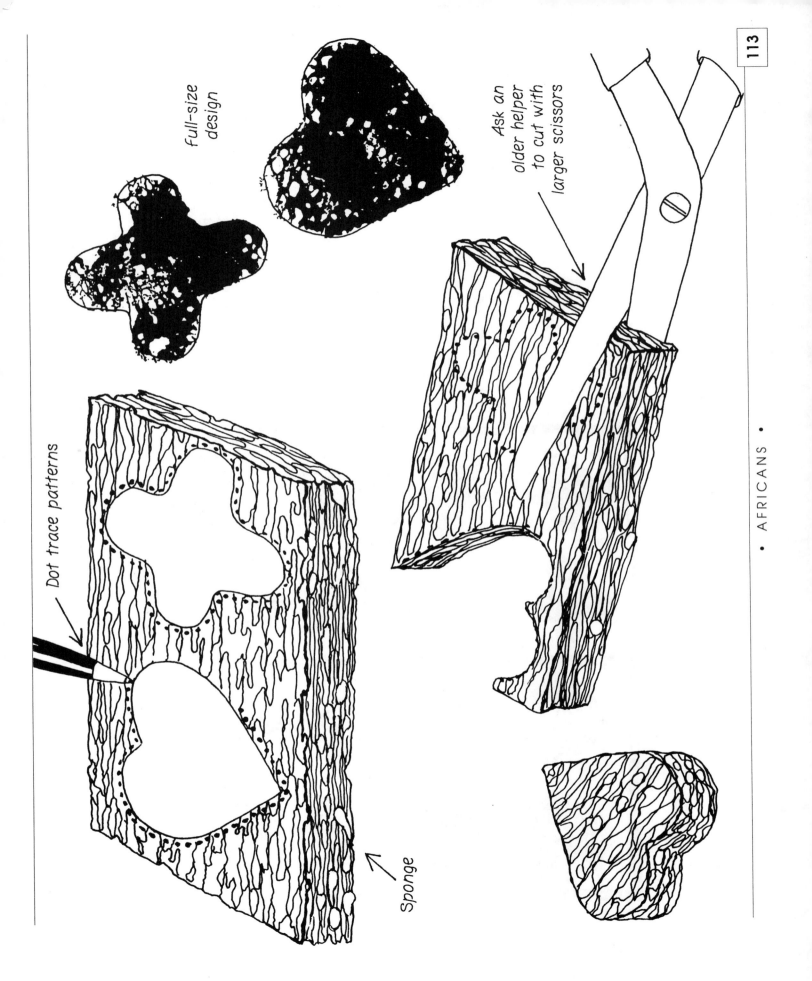

full-size design

Dot trace patterns

Sponge

Ask an older helper to cut with larger scissors

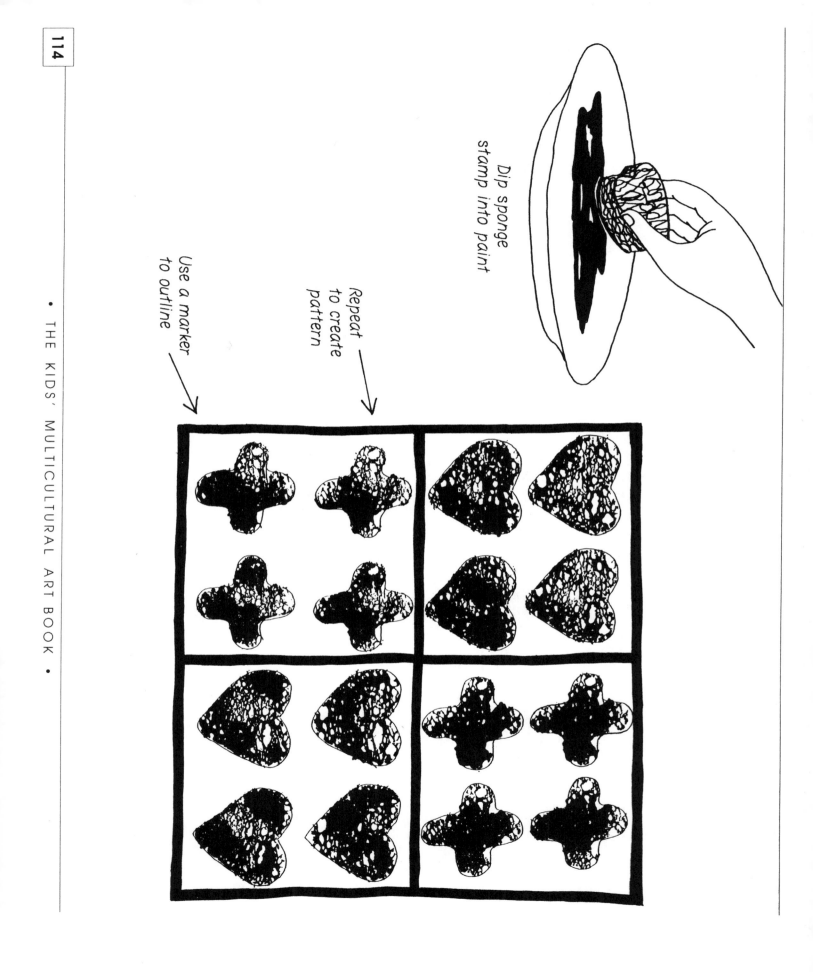

Dip sponge
stamp into paint

Repeat
to create
pattern

Use a marker
to outline

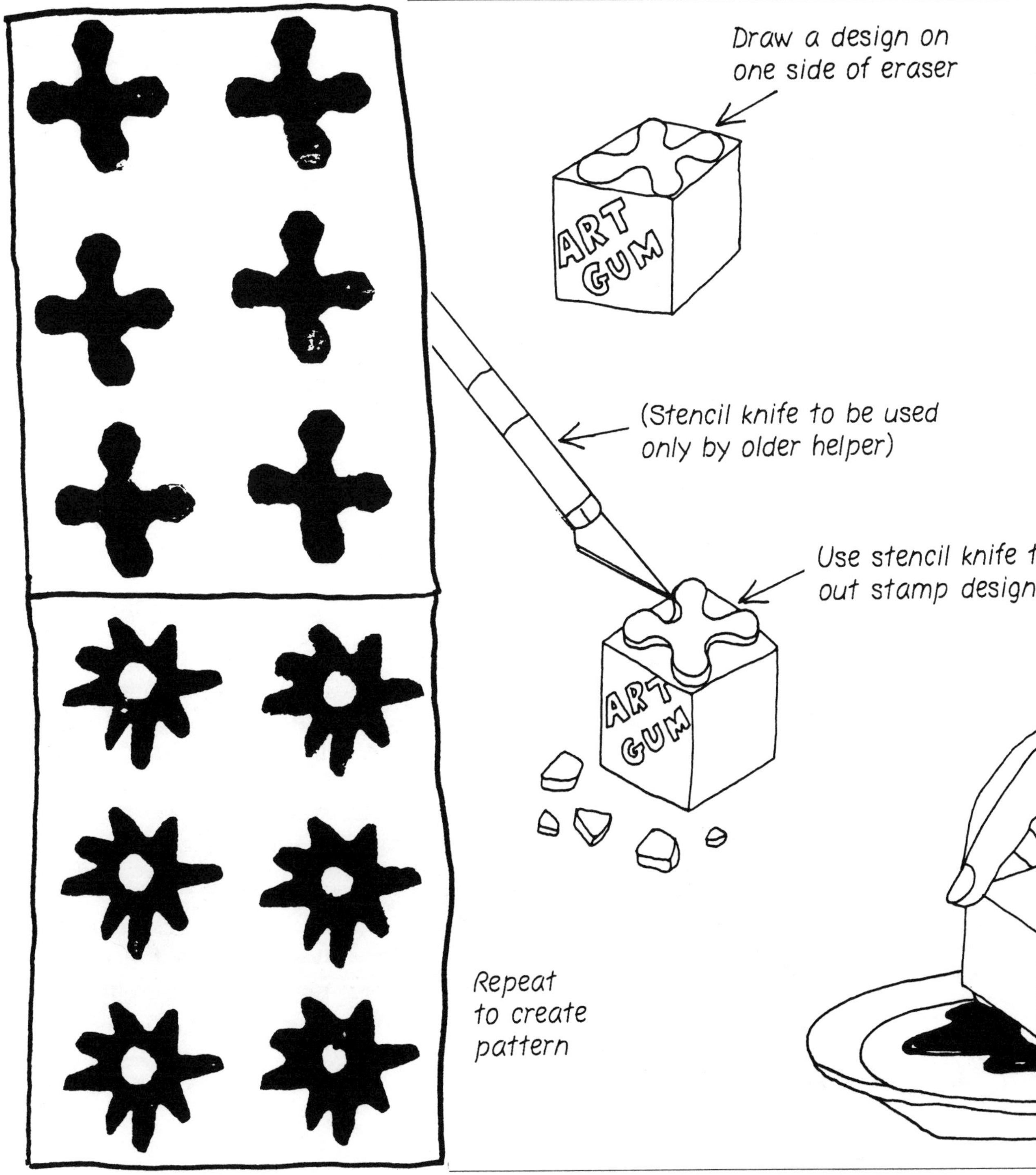

Art Works! ☐

☐ ☐ A roll of any plain paper can be stamped and used to make special gift wrap. (Let the stamped design dry before wrapping anything.)

UNITY

PRAISE

FAITH

Draw a design on one side of eraser

(Stencil knife to be used only by older helper)

Use stencil knife to cut out stamp design

ART GUM

ART GUM

Dip stamp into paint

Repeat to create pattern

KORHOGO MUD CLOTH

The Korhogo of the Ivory Coast and the Bamana of Mali use similar methods when making their decorative mud cloths. These artists paint designs on handwoven cotton cloth with mud that has been collected, placed in a clay pot, covered with water, and left to sit for a year.

◆ MATERIALS ◆

Piece of cotton muslin, raw cotton canvas, or any white cotton cloth, like an old sheet, about 9" x 12" or any other size

Mud, cleaned, about 1 cup

Wire mesh strainer
(or a piece of window screen)

Brown and blue tempera paint

Small coffee can with plastic lid, small containers

Spoon, pencil, paintbrush, wooden tongue depressor, small tree branch or twig

To clean the mud:

1 Dig up about one cup of mud, or use dirt if the earth is dry.

2 Working at a sink, place the wire mesh strainer over the coffee can. Pour a little mud or dirt onto the strainer and run water over it. Throw away any debris in the strainer outside.

3 The mud will sink to the bottom of the can, leaving a layer of water on top. Pour off some of this water. Repeat the straining process until the mud is clean.

To make the mud and paint mixture:

1 Add about ½ cup brown and ½ cup blue tempera paint to the cleaned mud in can. Stir well. This makes enough for several mud cloths.

Making a mud cloth:

1 Draw your design and border in pencil on the cotton cloth. Zigzag borders or triangle shapes look good. Double line the pencil drawing to make painting easier.

2 Scoop a small amount of mud paint into a bowl.

3 Using a variety of tools, apply the mud paint to your design. Along with a paintbrush, try using a small tree branch or sharp twig, or a wooden tongue depressor that has been cut to a point on one end. This makes very thin lines.

4 Cover the coffee can to store the mud paint. If it dries out, just add a little water. Make several mud cloths and hang them on a string using clothespins, or use thumbtacks to hang them on a wall.

Turtle and bird designs

Border designs

Korhogo
mud cloth
design. Use
this one
or make
up one of
your own

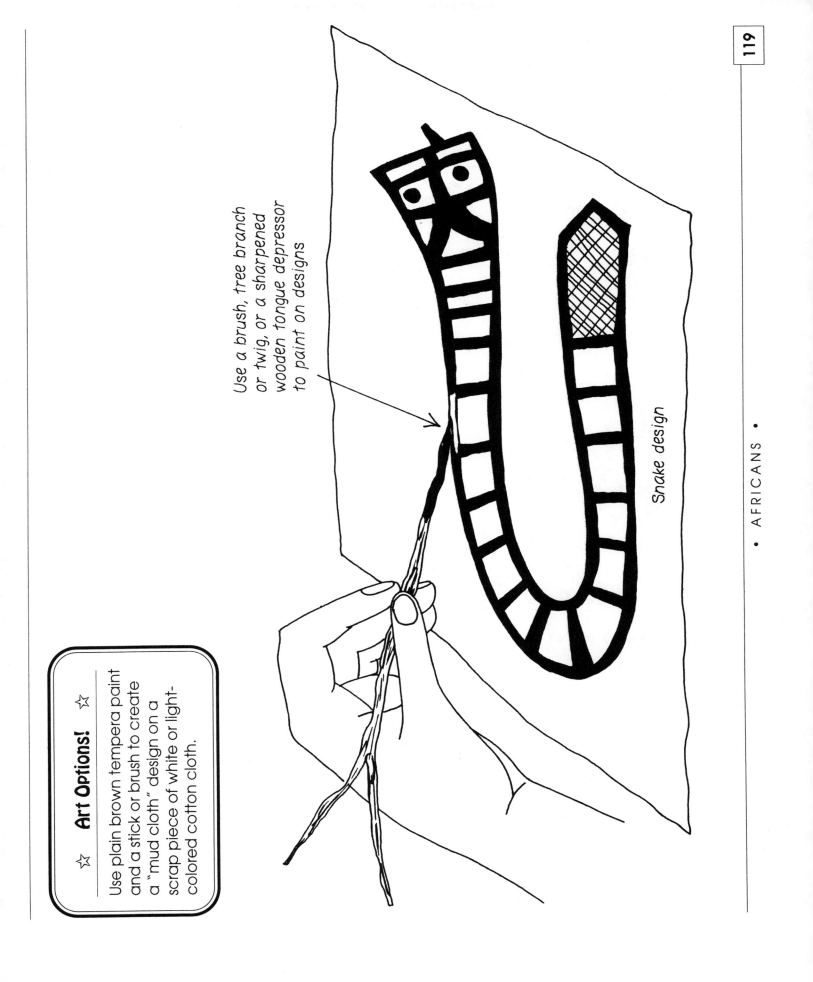

Use a brush, tree branch
or twig, or a sharpened
wooden tongue depressor
to paint on designs

Snake design

☆ **Art Options!** ☆

Use plain brown tempera paint
and a stick or brush to create
a "mud cloth" design on a
scrap piece of white or light-
colored cotton cloth.

• AFRICANS •

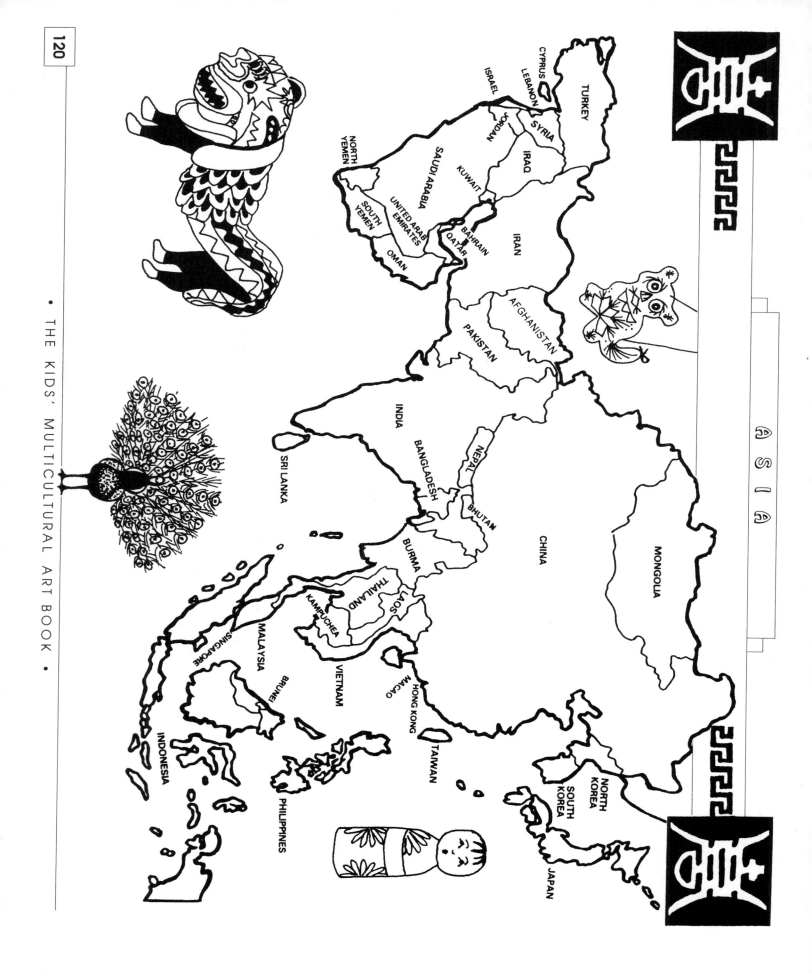

• THE KIDS' MULTICULTURAL ART BOOK •

ASIA

TURKEY

CYPRUS
LEBANON
ISRAEL
JORDAN
SYRIA
IRAQ
KUWAIT
NORTH YEMEN
SAUDI ARABIA
SOUTH YEMEN
UNITED ARAB EMIRATES
BAHRAIN
QATAR
OMAN
IRAN
AFGHANISTAN
PAKISTAN
INDIA
NEPAL
BHUTAN
BANGLADESH
BURMA
SRI LANKA
THAILAND
LAOS
VIETNAM
KAMPUCHEA
MALAYSIA
SINGAPORE
BRUNEI
INDONESIA
PHILIPPINES
CHINA
MONGOLIA
MACAO
HONG KONG
TAIWAN
NORTH KOREA
SOUTH KOREA
JAPAN

ASIANS

INDIA, THE FAR EAST, & THE SOUTHEAST

If you look at a map of our world, you'll notice how enormous Asia is. That's because Asia is the largest continent on Earth! So as you might expect, there are many different groups of people living there — each with a rich cultural identity and language all its own!

These Asian countries may seem a world away, but it's possible to bring their cultures right into your home by recreating the same traditional arts and crafts that they make. How will making your own ethnic creations from this part of the world help you understand these exciting cultures? Well, when you make these artifacts, you'll be sharing things that have special meaning and are a part of people's daily lives.

Have you ever eaten Chinese, Indian, or Thai food? It's delicious, isn't it? Far

East countries have influenced millions of people all over the world with their food and their arts. Although Asian countries such as China, Japan, Vietnam, and Korea have different languages, cultures, and traditions, they do have in common an appreciation for their native arts and crafts. You'll understand how meaningful age-old handicrafts and folk arts are in China when you create your own *Good Luck Dragon* (page 142), or your own *Thai Hanging Owl* (page 148).

Whether you are making a *Uchiwa* (page 136) or a *Folding Photo Screen* (page 138), you'll come to appreciate the Japanese artistic tradition of simplicity and beauty. Or you may be interested in the handmade gifts for children such as the *Twirling Palm Puppet* (page 124) or the Japanese *Kokeshi Doll* (page 134). In each case, you will begin to understand how unique each Asian culture's folk art tradition is — and you will be having a lot of fun exploring your own creativity, too — as you re-create these age-old folk arts and crafts.

INDIA

TWIRLING PALM PUPPET

In India, crafters shape a dried palm from the palm tree into puppets that are placed on a stick and twirled between the palms of the hands. The puppet's arms and legs jump out as it is twirled. This is called a "palm" puppet for two reasons then!

◆ MATERIALS ◆

Scrap paper

White poster board: 3" x 8", 3" x 4", 4" x 4"

Drinking straw

Paper fasteners, 4

Black marker, pencil, stapler, scissors

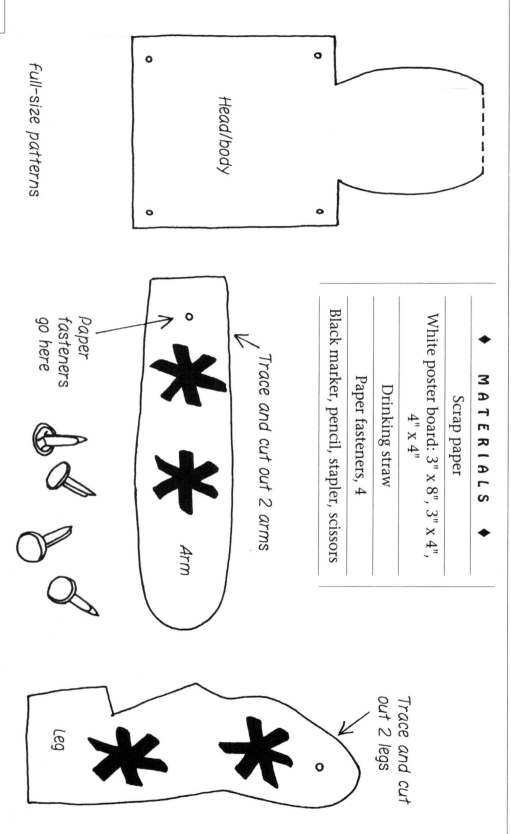

full-size patterns

Head/body

Paper fasteners go here

Arm

Trace and cut out 2 arms

Leg

Trace and cut out 2 legs

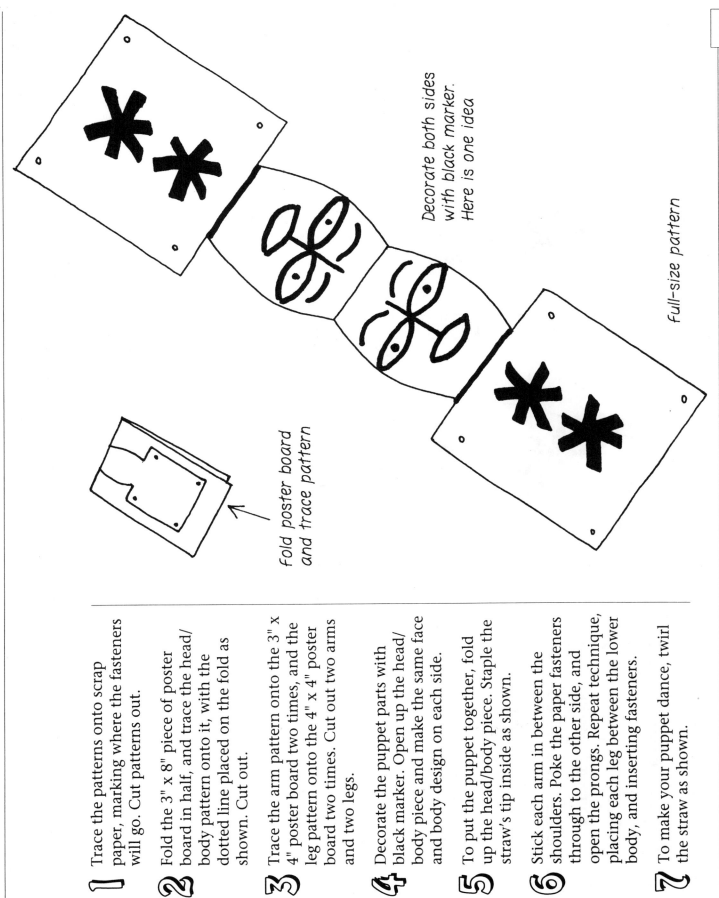

Decorate both sides with black marker. Here is one idea

Fold poster board and trace pattern

Full-size pattern

1 Trace the patterns onto scrap paper, marking where the fasteners will go. Cut patterns out.

2 Fold the 3" x 8" piece of poster board in half, and trace the head/body pattern onto it, with the dotted line placed on the fold as shown. Cut out.

3 Trace the arm pattern onto the 3" x 4" poster board two times, and the leg pattern onto the 4" x 4" poster board two times. Cut out two arms and two legs.

4 Decorate the puppet parts with black marker. Open up the head/body piece and make the same face and body design on each side.

5 To put the puppet together, fold up the head/body piece. Staple the straw's tip inside as shown.

6 Stick each arm in between the shoulders. Poke the paper fasteners through to the other side, and open the prongs. Repeat technique, placing each leg between the lower body, and inserting fasteners.

7 To make your puppet dance, twirl the straw as shown.

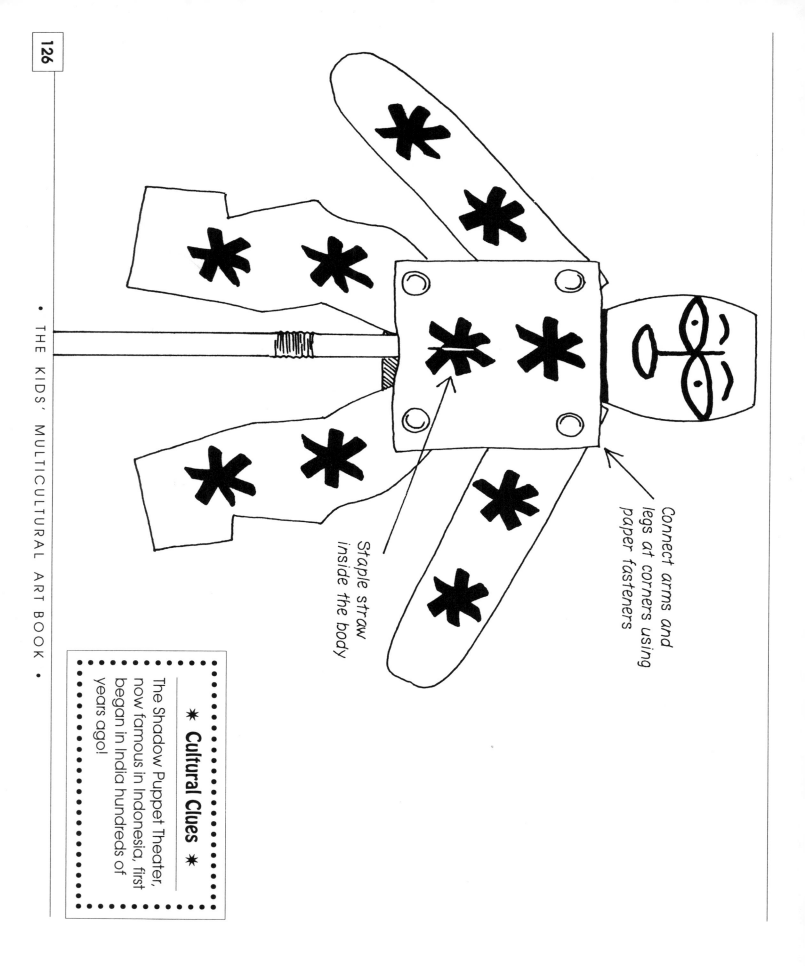

Connect arms and
legs at corners using
paper fasteners

Staple straw
inside the body

✻ Cultural Clues ✻

The Shadow Puppet Theater,
now famous in Indonesia, first
began in India hundreds of
years ago!

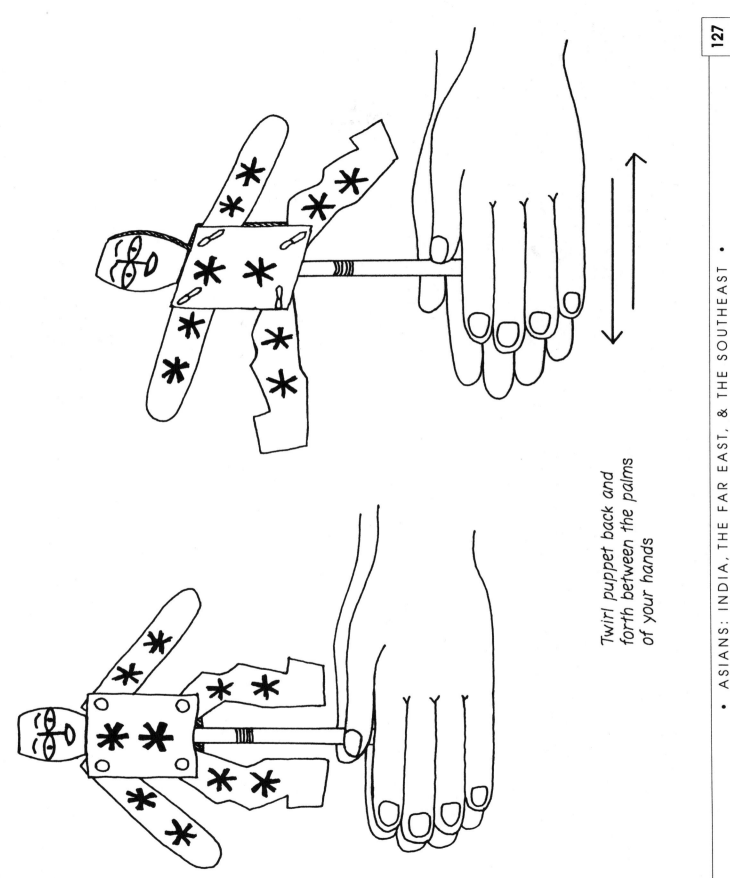

Twirl puppet back and forth between the palms of your hands

I N D I A

PEACOCK OF INDIA

The national bird of India is the magnificent peacock. The feathers of the male peacock have "eye" designs of golden orange and blue-green that are seen when he raises his train of feathers in a grand display.

◆ **M A T E R I A L S** ◆

White paper plate, 9"

Construction paper: 5" x 9" in blue; 2" x 3" in orange; small white scrap for beak

Scrap paper

Markers in dark colors

Tempera paint, orange and blue, on small plate

Old pencil (use eraser end) or cotton swab

Pencil, tape, stapler, scissors

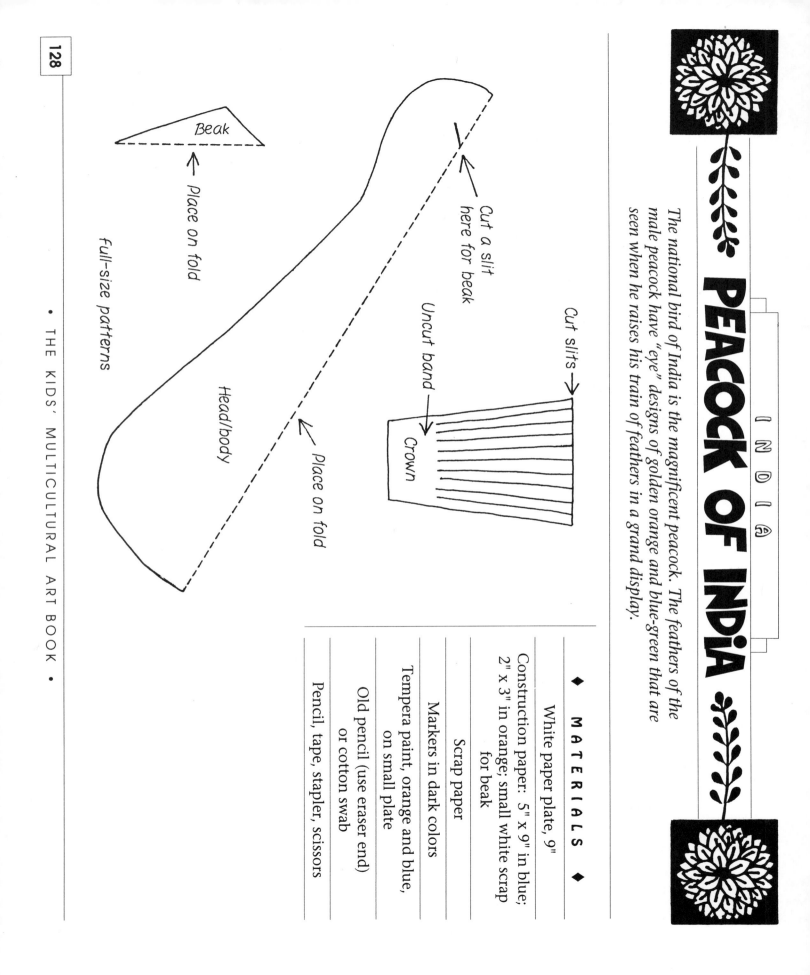

Cut slits →

Uncut band

Crown

Cut a slit here for beak

Place on fold

Head/body

Place on fold

Beak

↑ Place on fold

Full-size patterns

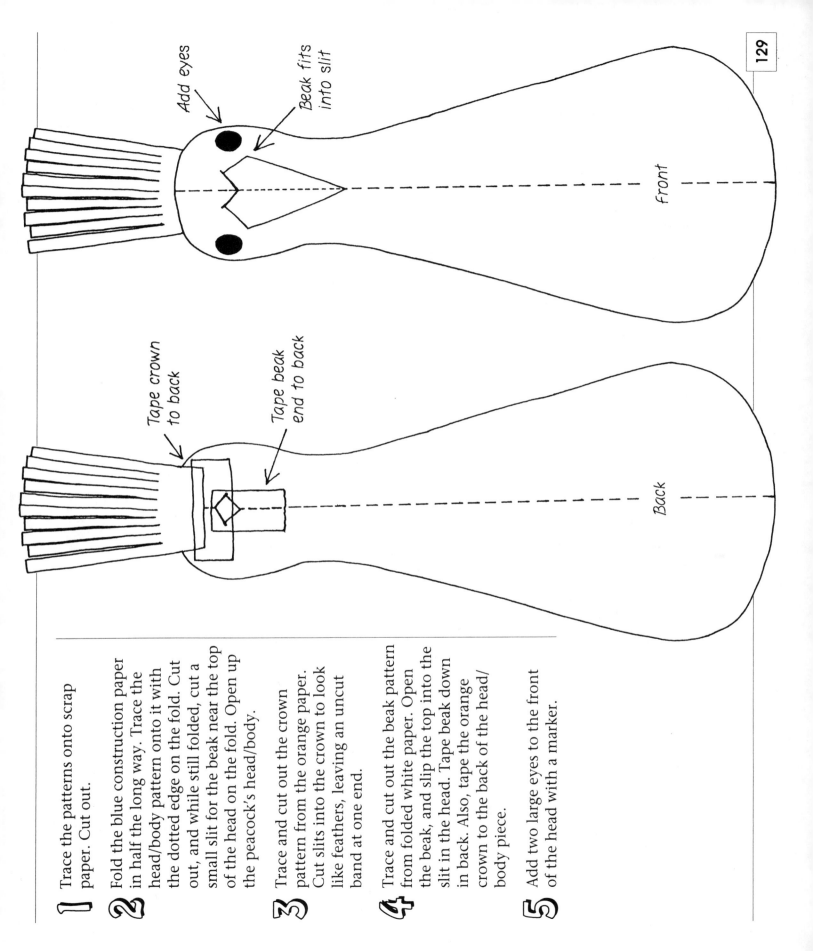

Add eyes

Beak fits into slit

Front

Tape crown to back

Tape beak end to back

Back

1 Trace the patterns onto scrap paper. Cut out.

2 Fold the blue construction paper in half the long way. Trace the head/body pattern onto it with the dotted edge on the fold. Cut out, and while still folded, cut a small slit for the beak near the top of the head on the fold. Open up the peacock's head/body.

3 Trace and cut out the crown pattern from the orange paper. Cut slits into the crown to look like feathers, leaving an uncut band at one end.

4 Trace and cut out the beak pattern from folded white paper. Open the beak, and slip the top into the slit in the head. Tape beak down in back. Also, tape the orange crown to the back of the head/body piece.

5 Add two large eyes to the front of the head with a marker.

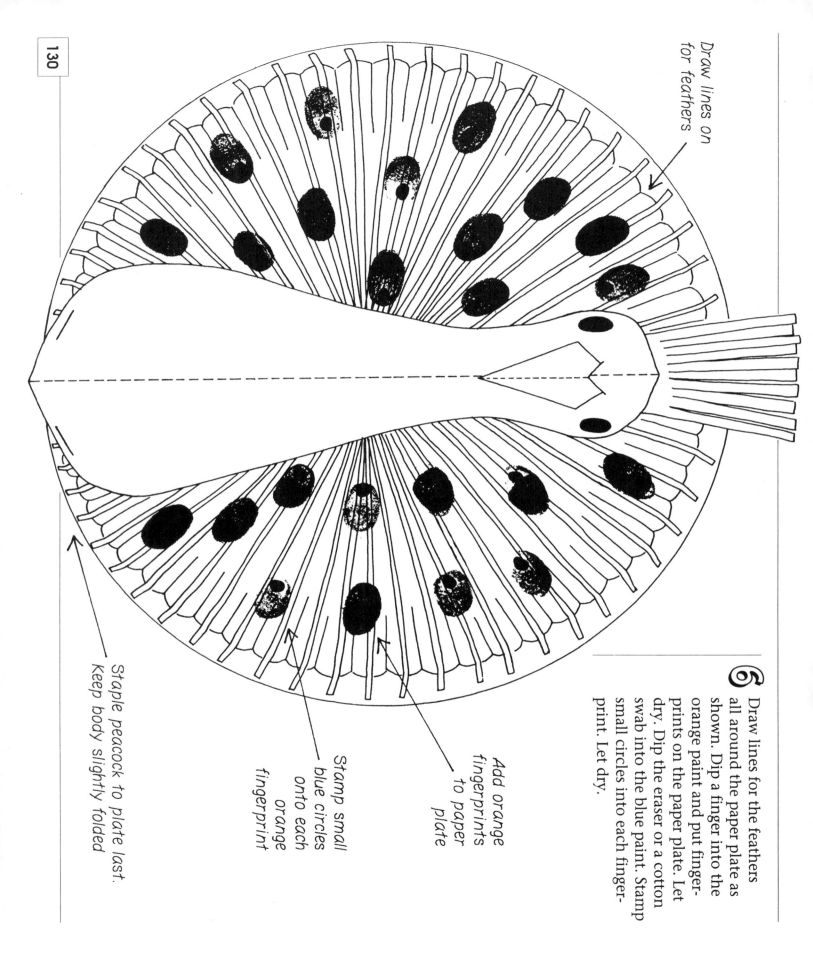

Draw lines on
for feathers

6 Draw lines for the feathers
all around the paper plate as
shown. Dip a finger into the
orange paint and put fingerprints on the paper plate. Let
dry. Dip the eraser or a cotton
swab into the blue paint. Stamp
small circles into each fingerprint. Let dry.

Add orange
fingerprints
to paper
plate

Stamp small
blue circles
onto each
orange
fingerprint

Staple peacock to plate last.
Keep body slightly folded

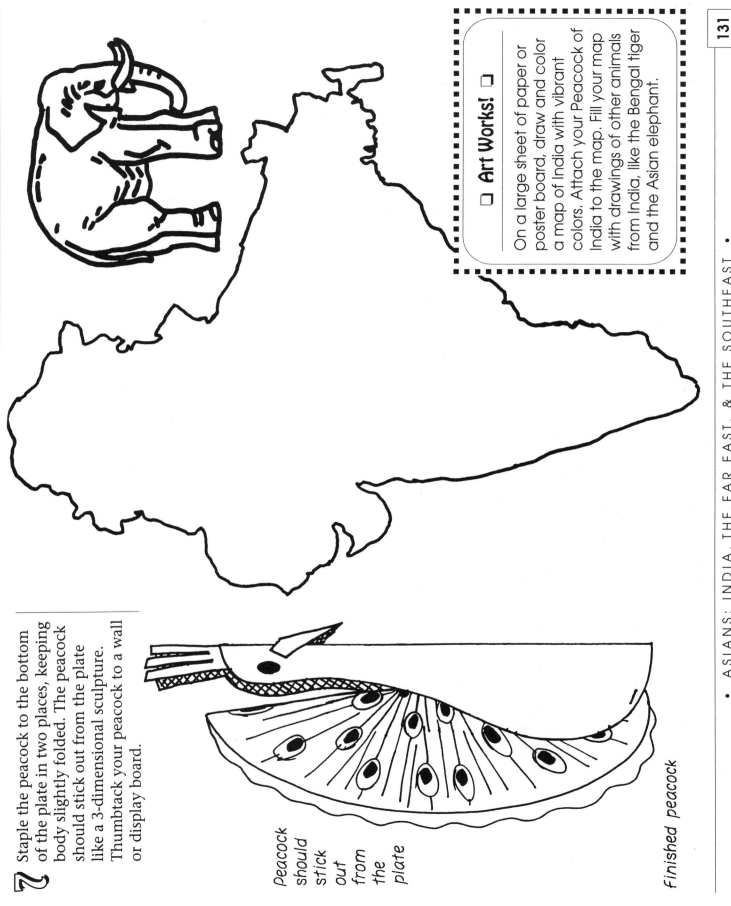

7 Staple the peacock to the bottom of the plate in two places, keeping body slightly folded. The peacock should stick out from the plate like a 3-dimensional sculpture. Thumbtack your peacock to a wall or display board.

Peacock should stick out from the plate

Finished peacock

□ **Art Works!** □

On a large sheet of paper or poster board, draw and color a map of India with vibrant colors. Attach your Peacock of India to the map. Fill your map with drawings of other animals from India, like the Bengal tiger and the Asian elephant.

PAPER EGG FiGURiNE

On Japan's Children's Day (May 5), a boy might receive a real eggshell figurine from his parents (who hope their son will grow up to be strong). Give your paper figurine as a gift with a special message dressed like Japanese heroes. These figurines are often hung around its neck. Or, put it next to a bouquet of flowers or on a shelf.

◆ **M A T E R I A L S** ◆

White paper, 8½" x 11"

Small piece of yarn, about 6" long

Small scrap of paper

Pencil, crayons or markers, stapler, scissors, hole punch

1 Trace the doll pattern onto the white paper, and cut out.

2 Color with crayons or markers as shown, or make up your own design. Overlap the ends around the back and staple closed. Fold the sleeves toward the front.

3 On a small scrap of paper, write a message or draw a picture. Punch a hole at each end of the top and pass the yarn through the holes. Tie ends together and hang on your paper egg figure.

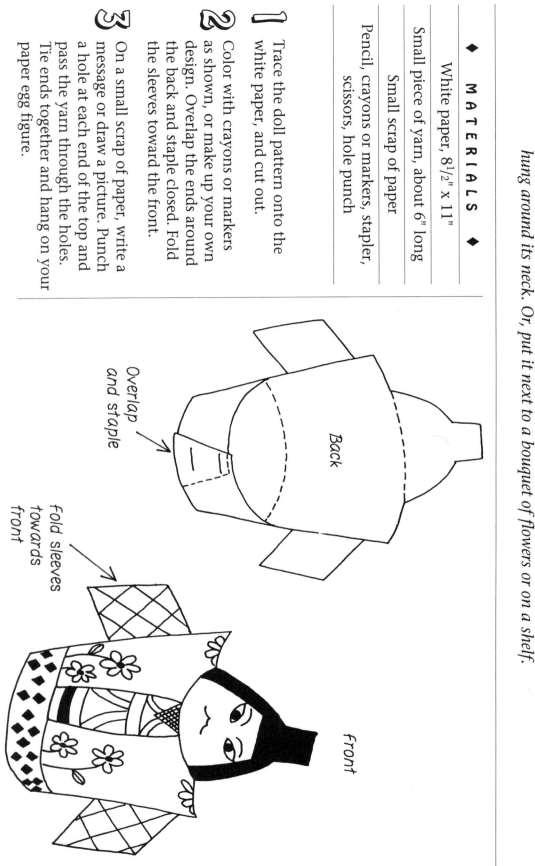

Back

Overlap
and staple

fold sleeves
towards
front

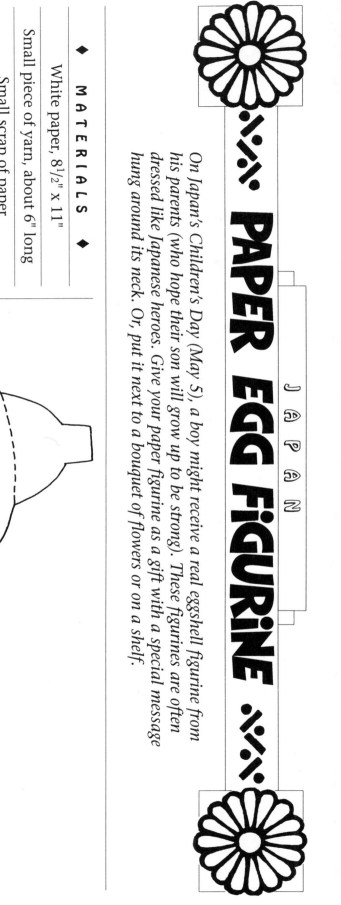

front

☆ **Art Options!** ☆

Make other paper egg figures by changing the pattern or color on its clothes. Make a little flag, and glue it to a toothpick. Attach the flag to one of the sleeves.

Hang this on your paper egg figure

HAPPY SPRING

Decorate with magic marker or crayons

Trace and cut out

Full-size pattern

KOKESHI DOLL

Dolls are an important part of many Japanese festivals. One type of doll, the kokeshi (ko-KE-shee), is made of a long, round piece of wood, usually from the dogwood tree, and has a large, round head. Kokeshi dolls have no arms or legs, and their faces, hair, and clothing are all painted on with bright colors.

◆ MATERIALS ◆

Cardboard tube from toilet paper (or paper towel tube, cut in half)

Ball, about 3" (made from used aluminum foil)

Papier-mache mixture (see page 152 for recipe) in bowl

Newspaper strips

Tempera paint in small cups: white or light color; black or dark color

Acrylic gloss varnish

Printed origami or wrapping paper, about 5" x 7"

Construction paper, any color, 1/2" x 7" strip for sash

Small piece of string or yarn

Paintbrushes, pencil, glue, scissors

Copy pattern onto printed origami or wrapping paper

Full-size patterns

Kimono

Sash

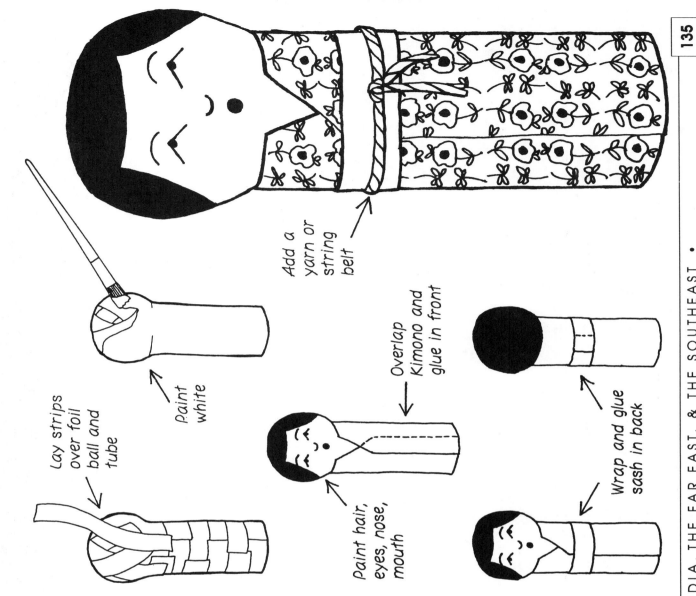

Lay strips over foil ball and tube

Paint white

Add a yarn or string belt

Overlap Kimono and glue in front

Paint hair, eyes, nose, mouth

Wrap and glue sash in back

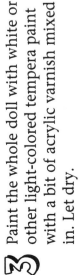

1. Glue the foil ball to one end of the cardboard tube.

2. Follow the instructions for covering the paper tube and foil ball completely with papier-mache paste and newspaper strips on page 152. Dry overnight.

3. Paint the whole doll with white or other light-colored tempera paint with a bit of acrylic varnish mixed in. Let dry.

4. Mix a small amount of black or other dark-colored paint with a little acrylic varnish. Paint on the hair, eyes, nose, and mouth as shown. Let dry.

5. Draw the kimono pattern onto the printed paper and cut out. Wrap the kimono around the doll, overlap the front, and glue in place as shown. Make a construction paper sash and wrap around the doll's waist. Glue it down in the back. Tie a small piece of yarn around the sash for the belt.

J A P A N

PAPER UCHIWA

The Japanese fan themselves with paper fans called uchiwa (OO-chee-wah), made of split bamboo and washi (WASH-ee), Japanese paper. Stenciled designs make the fans especially beautiful. Keep cool with your own hand-powered cooler made out of poster board and a wooden tongue depressor.

◆ M A T E R I A L S ◆

White or any light-colored poster board, 7" x 7"

Scrap paper

Wooden tongue depressor

Pencil, markers, scissors, stapler

1 Draw a fan onto the poster board, using almost the whole piece, and cut out. Staple the tongue depressor to the fan as shown.

2 Turn the fan over and decorate with markers. Remember to keep the design simple!

These are Japanese designs. Copy these or make up your own

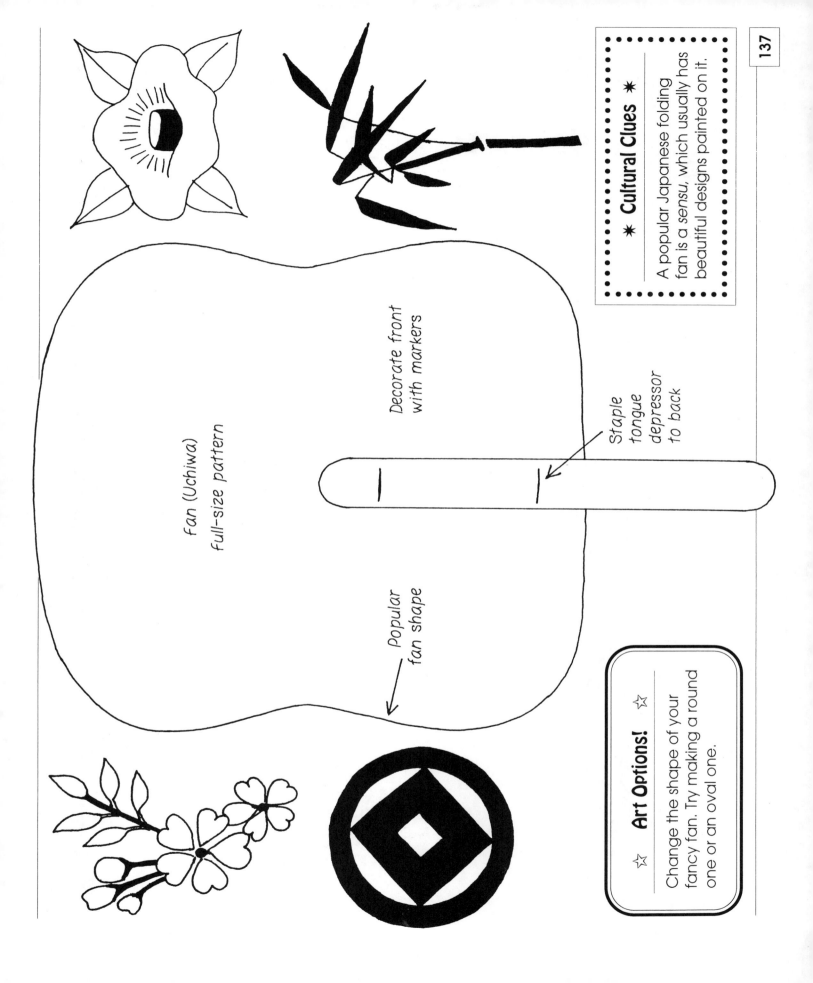

Fan (Uchiwa)
full-size pattern

Decorate front
with markers

Staple
tongue
depressor
to back

Popular
fan shape

✳ **Cultural Clues** ✳

A popular Japanese folding
fan is a *sensu*, which usually has
beautiful designs painted on it.

JAPAN

JAPANESE FOLDING SCREEN

Japanese artists make the loveliest folding screens, carved with designs and painted black. Some are made from wood frames and have hand-painted silk stretched in each panel. The paintings are often of flowers, such as peonies, or landscapes. The Japanese also have a love for things that are very small, so miniature table top screens are a popular decoration. Make a paper folding screen to hold your favorite photos. Pick out four special photos. What a great gift! I made one and gave it to my son. It includes everyone in the family plus our dog!

Fold in half

fold half
toward
back fold

flip over and
fold half toward
center fold

Draw and
cut out
4 shapes

Tape a photo
over each
opening
on back

Decorate front with markers

◆ M A T E R I A L S ◆

White poster board, 2 pieces, 9" x 12"

Photos, 4

Markers, many colors

Pencil, tape, glue, scissors

1 Fold one piece of poster board in half. Fold one side in half toward the back fold as shown. Flip the poster board over, and fold the other side in half toward the back fold. It should look accordion-style. Repeat with the other piece of poster board.

2 Take one folded poster board, and draw any shapes you like in each of its four panels. Cut out each shape to create four openings.

3 Tape a photo over each opening, making sure the photo is larger than the opening and centered.

4 Glue the other folded poster board onto the back of the piece with the photos taped down, making a stronger backing. Press these together. Refold the screen to get the creases back.

5 Lay the screen on a table and use the markers to create designs of your choice. Use flowers as the Japanese do or be as creative as you like!

KOREAN DRAGON PUPPET

Long ago, Koreans believed the blue dragon would protect them from the east. (The white tiger was said to protect Korea from the west.) This is why the blue dragon is on the east side of many of Korea's 7,000 temples! Dragons are make believe, of course, but you can turn a brown paper bag into a blue dragon in no time at all!

◆ **M A T E R I A L S** ◆

Blue construction paper, about 5" x 7"

Construction paper, 2" square, any other color

Brown paper lunch bag

Cotton balls, 2

Markers, blue and black

Pencil, glue, scissors

1. Draw the spine, crown, teeth, and tongue on the blue construction paper. Cut out. Cut a triangle out of another color paper for the nose.

2. Color the whole bag blue.

3. Glue the crown, teeth, and tongue on the bottom part of the paper bag that will be the head, as shown. Glue on the cotton ball eyes and the triangle nose. Add two large nose dots with a black marker.

4. Fold the straight edge of the spine over about 1/2". Glue this folded part to the middle back of the bag. Lift up the spine so that the points stand up.

5. Draw scales on the front and back of the dragon with black marker. Then, draw the four claws on each foot on the bottom front.

6. Slip your hand into the puppet and wave your fingers up and down to move the head.

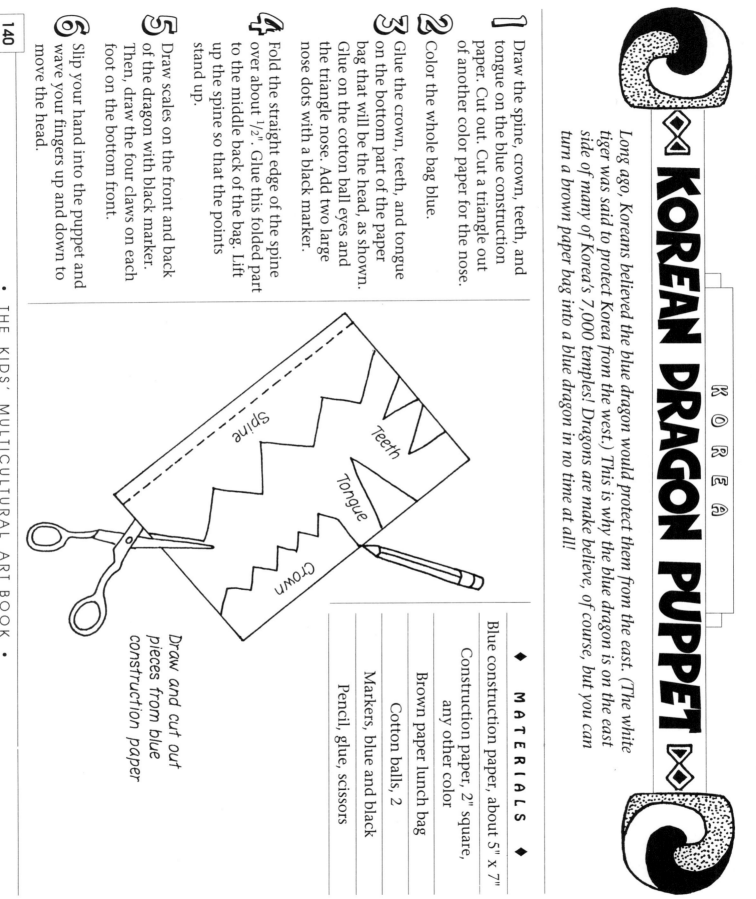

Draw and cut out pieces from blue construction paper

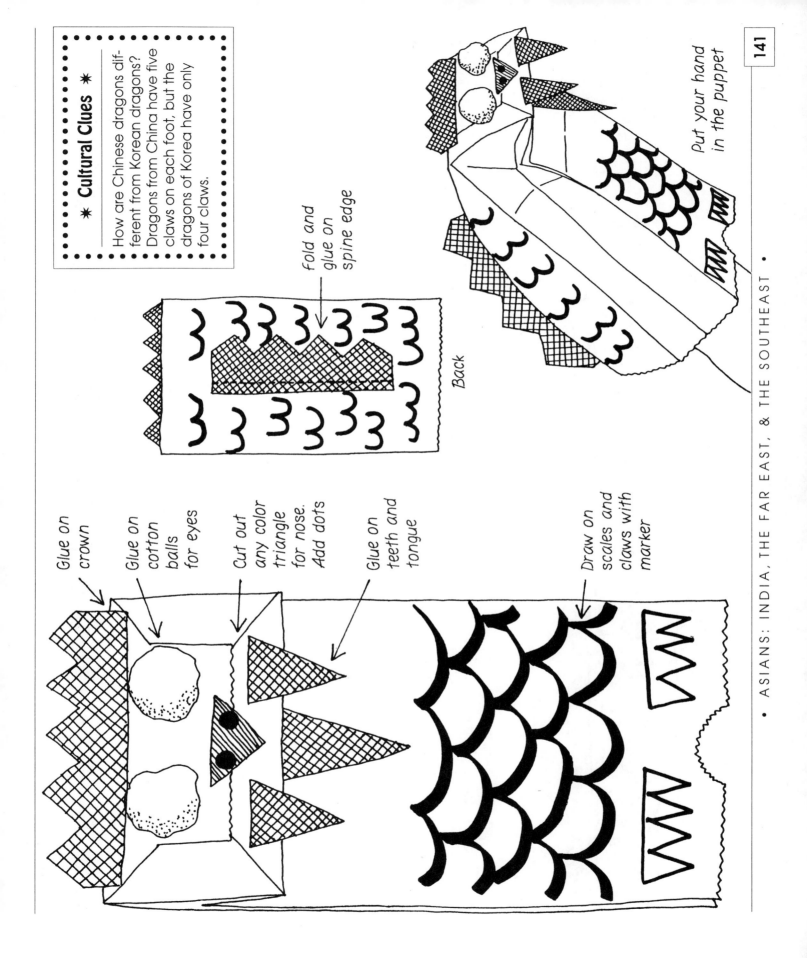

★ Cultural Clues ★

How are Chinese dragons different from Korean dragons? Dragons from China have five claws on each foot, but the dragons of Korea have only four claws.

Fold and glue on spine edge

Back

Glue on crown

Glue on cotton balls for eyes

Cut out any color triangle for nose. Add dots

Glue on teeth and tongue

Draw on scales and claws with marker

Put your hand in the puppet

• ASIANS: INDIA, THE FAR EAST, & THE SOUTHEAST •

GOOD LUCK DRAGON

The dragon is a make-believe creature that has been a part of Chinese culture for thousands of years. Chinese New Year parades always feature a fierce dragon with a large gold and red head and a very long, costumed body. Underneath men dance and move so that the glorious dragon comes to life!

1. To form the mouth, cut wide slits into each side of the paper cup as shown. Then, tape the cup to one end of the paper tube.

2. Cut out two egg carton sections for the dragon's feet and glue them to the tube. Let dry.

3. Cut out three humps from the center section of the egg carton and tape this to the dragon's back, as shown.

4. Form the tail with some scrap aluminum foil. Tape an arrowhead shape cut from the cardboard scrap to the foil tail. Stick the other end of the foil tail into the paper tube and tape in place.

5. Follow the instruction on page 152 to completely cover the dragon's form (tail, humps, feet — everything) with papier-mache paste and newspaper strips. Dry overnight.

6. Trim off any extra newspaper around the feet. Paint the dragon any color you wish with tempera paint mixed with a little acrylic gloss varnish. When the body is dry, paint on scales, eyes, a nose and claws with other colors. Let dry.

7. To make teeth, glue two toothpicks to the front of the mouth at the top. Tape in place until the glue dries; then remove tape.

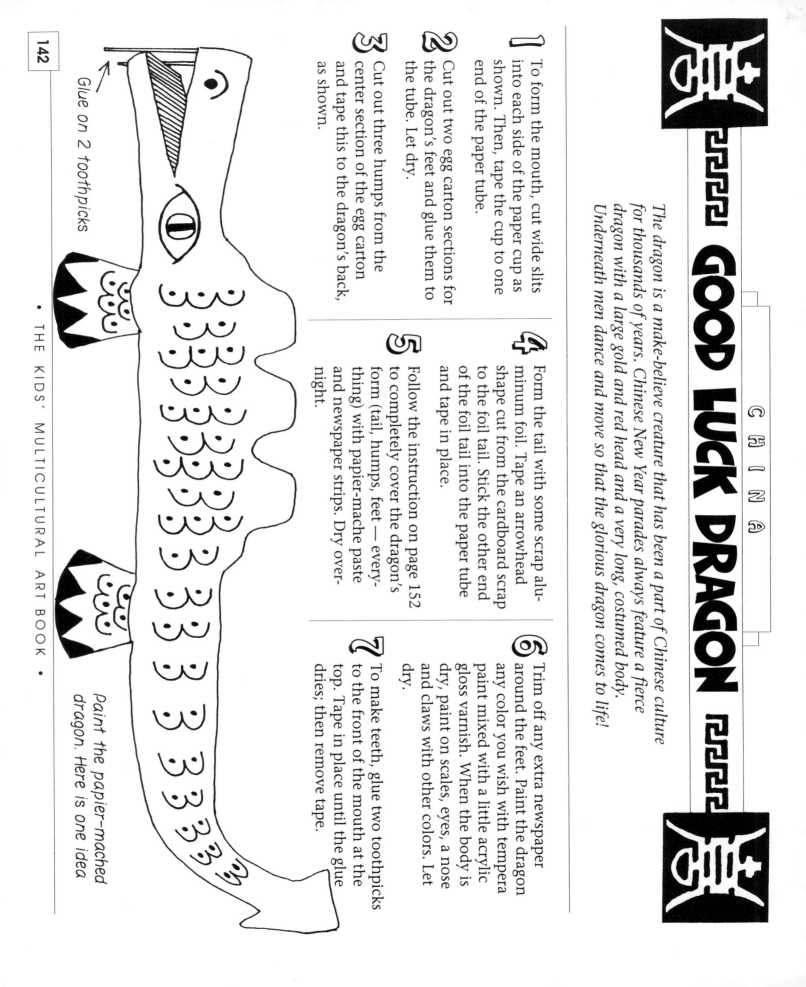

Glue on 2 toothpicks

Paint the papier-mached dragon. Here is one idea

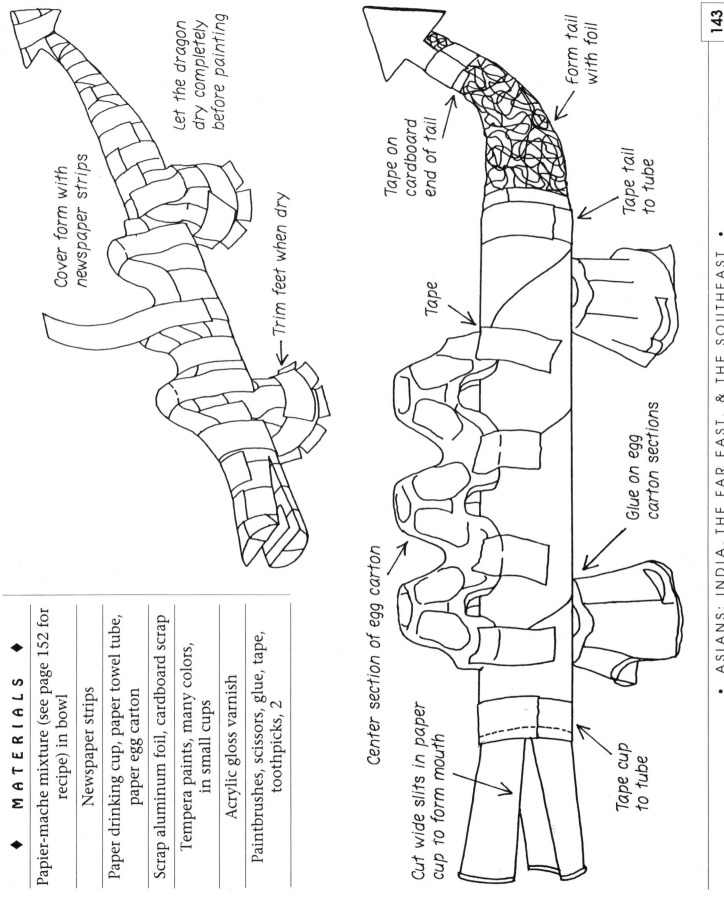

♦ MATERIALS ♦

Papier-mache mixture (see page 152 for recipe) in bowl

Newspaper strips

Paper drinking cup, paper towel tube, paper egg carton

Scrap aluminum foil, cardboard scrap

Tempera paints, many colors, in small cups

Acrylic gloss varnish

Paintbrushes, scissors, glue, tape, toothpicks, 2

Cover form with newspaper strips

Let the dragon dry completely before painting

Trim feet when dry

Tape on cardboard end of tail

form tail with foil

Tape

Tape tail to tube

Center section of egg carton

Glue on egg carton sections

Cut wide slits in paper cup to form mouth

Tape cup to tube

CHINA

CHINESE EGG PAINTING

What better place to paint a picture than on an egg! Just think of an eggshell as a perfect piece of blank paper. Chinese egg painting — an ancient tradition still in use today — was so special that they put painted eggs in temples, or holy buildings, as an offering to God.

◆ MATERIALS ◆

White chicken egg

Watercolor paints, cup of water, small paintbrush

Paper clip, small bowl

Milk bottle cap
(or small plastic or wood ring)

Pencil, glue

1. Open the paper clip so that you have a long, straight piece. With the wide end of the egg up, gently tap an opening in the egg using the clip's sharp end. Be careful not to crack the whole egg.

2. Empty the insides into a small bowl. Refrigerate the egg to cook later (look for a recipe for Egg Drop Soup). Dry the outside of the egg.

3. Glue the eggshell, broken side down, onto the bottle cap. Let dry.

4. Lightly draw a design (as shown or make up your own) on the eggshell with a pencil.

5. Paint your egg with watercolors, keeping the painting light and open. Rinse the brush between each color. Let dry. (In Asian art, the background is not all covered with paint.)

6. Sign your eggshell painting with your initials in a small box shape as shown. This kind of signature or mark is known as a *chop* and is used by Chinese painters.

Here are some ideas. Use these or make up your own

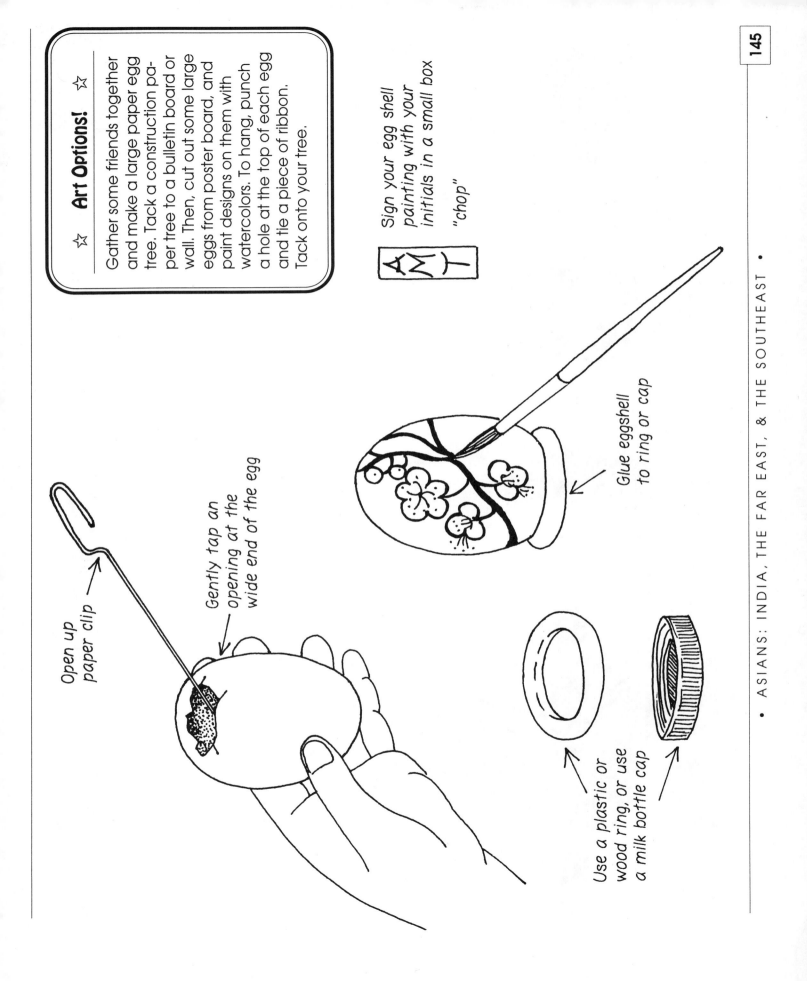

☆ **Art Options!** ☆

Gather some friends together and make a large paper egg tree. Tack a construction paper tree to a bulletin board or wall. Then, cut out some large eggs from poster board, and paint designs on them with watercolors. To hang, punch a hole at the top of each egg and tie a piece of ribbon. Tack onto your tree.

Sign your egg shell painting with your initials in a small box

"chop"

Glue eggshell to ring or cap

Open up paper clip

Gently tap an opening at the wide end of the egg

Use a plastic or wood ring, or use a milk bottle cap

C H I N A

TRADITIONAL PAPERCUTS

The Chinese make delicate papercuts — a sign of good luck — for celebrations, festivals, and home decorations. Papercuts use designs of dragons, frogs, people, flowers, birds, or anything the artist wishes. Glue your papercuts onto a homemade card or gift to make it special.

◆ MATERIALS ◆

Construction paper, any dark colors, 9" x 12" sheets

Scrap paper

Pencil, glue, hole punch, scissors

1 Make up your own patterns or trace any of the patterns shown on scrap paper. Cut out.

fold paper in half

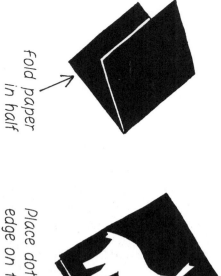

Place dotted line edge on fold

Trace pattern onto folded paper and cut out

2 Fold the construction paper in half. Place the dotted line edge of the pattern on the fold of the construction paper as shown. Trace the pattern on the construction paper and cut out.

3 Punch holes to create a design or add details like eyes wherever you wish. Open your papercut.

Punch holes to create designs or add details like eyes

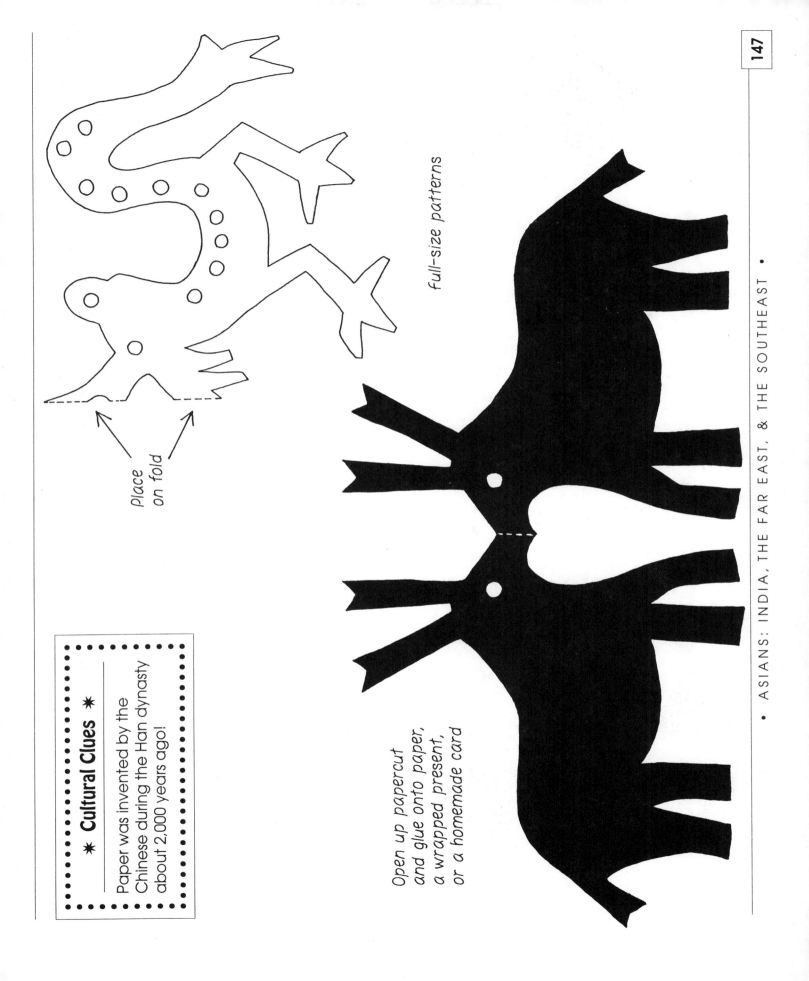

full-size patterns

Place on fold

✳ Cultural Clues ✳

Paper was invented by the Chinese during the Han dynasty about 2,000 years ago!

Open up papercut and glue onto paper, a wrapped present, or a homemade card

SOUTHEAST ASIA

THAi HANGING OWL

In Thailand, most children love flying kites of dragons, owls, other birds, and fishes. Kite contests, where one kite knocks another to the ground, are very popular.

You can make a hanging kite like those sold in Thailand's open-air markets. Hang yours by an open window and watch it float in the wind.

◆ MATERIALS ◆

White paper, 8 ½" x 11", 2 sheets

Markers in red, yellow, and black

Clothespins and string

Pencil, tape, scissors

1 Make two tracings of the owl half so they fit together to make a whole owl as shown. Connect the two pieces on the backside with tape. Cut out the owl.

2 Use the markers to decorate your owl any way you wish.

3 Make several owls and hang each with two clothespins on a line of string. It's a great room decoration!

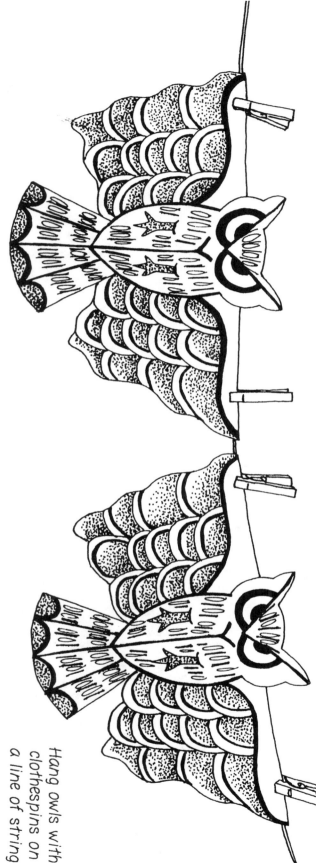

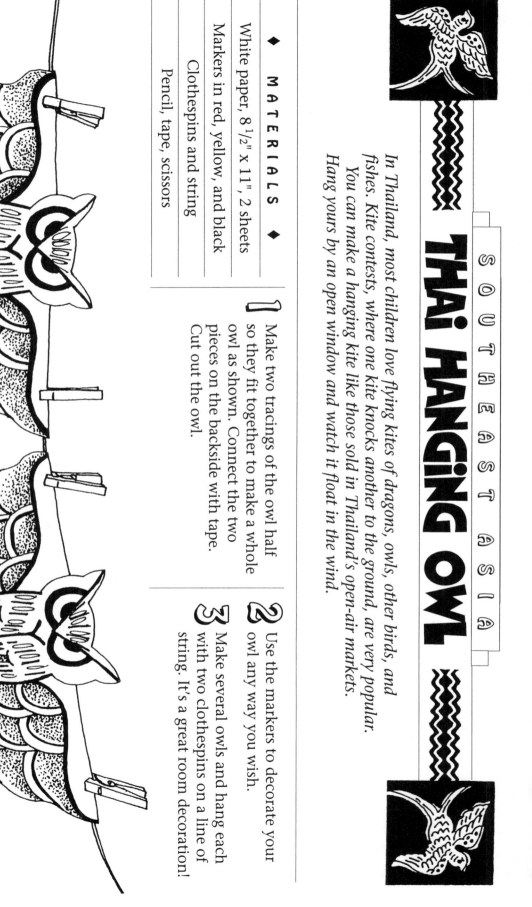

Hang owls with clothespins on a line of string

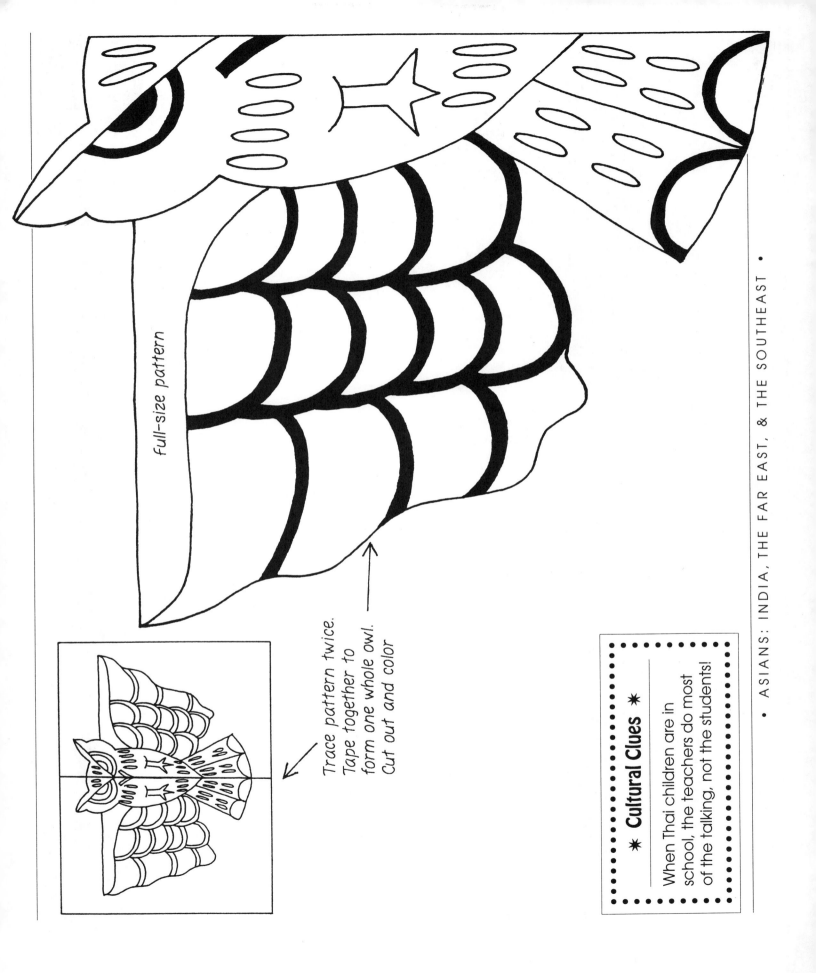

full-size pattern

Trace pattern twice.
Tape together to
form one whole owl.
Cut out and color

★ **Cultural Clues** ★

When Thai children are in
school, the teachers do most
of the talking, not the students!

VIETNAMESE DRAGON

The Dragon Dance, in which young men dance under a papier-mache and cloth dragon, is an exciting part of the colorful Tet festival parade, celebrating the Vietnamese New Year. Your Dancing Dragon is made from simple materials. Run and dance while holding it and watch the paper train fly in the wind!

◆ MATERIALS ◆

| Paper cup |
| Flexible straw |
| Construction paper, any color 1¹/₂" x 17" |
| Tape, scissors, hole punch |

1 To form the dragon's mouth, cut wide slits into each side of the paper cup as shown. Punch two eye holes on the top of the cup.

2 To make the handle, punch a hole at the bottom of the cup. Poke the straw through the hole, bend it toward the front, and tape the end down as shown.

3 Fold the construction paper strip accordion-style. Cut a rounded edge on one end, and tape it to the bottom of the cup.

4 Hold the Dancing Dragon in one hand and run!

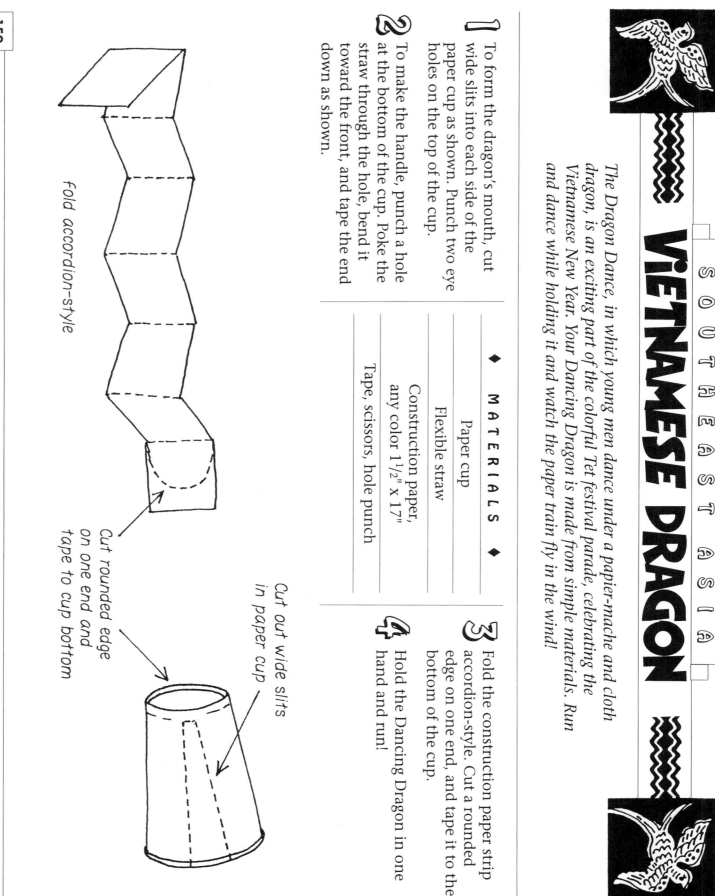

Fold accordion-style

Cut rounded edge on one end and tape to cup bottom

Cut out wide slits in paper cup

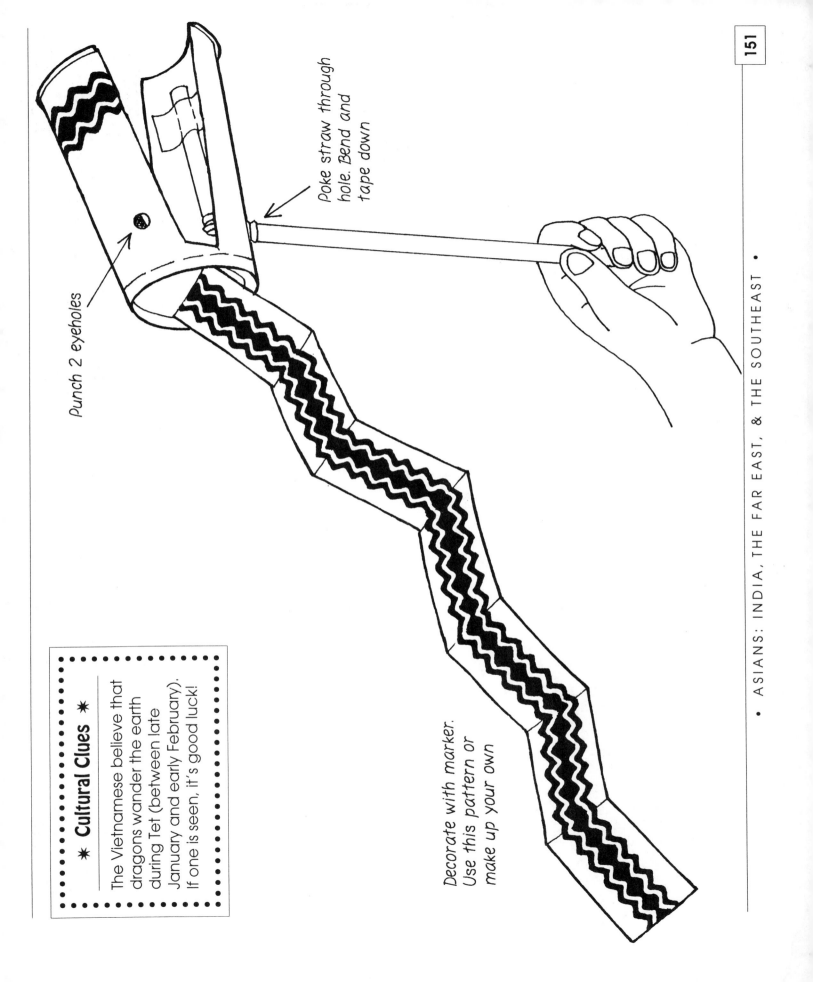

Punch 2 eyeholes

Poke straw through hole. Bend and tape down

✳ Cultural Clues ✳

The Vietnamese believe that dragons wander the earth during Tet (between late January and early February). If one is seen, it's good luck!

Decorate with marker. Use this pattern or make up your own

PAPiER-MACHE RECiPE

This homemade papier-mache (pa-per ma-SHAY) works as well as the powdered form found in many arts and crafts stores. This recipe makes very small batches. If you make too much, it's hard to save, so make more as you need it.

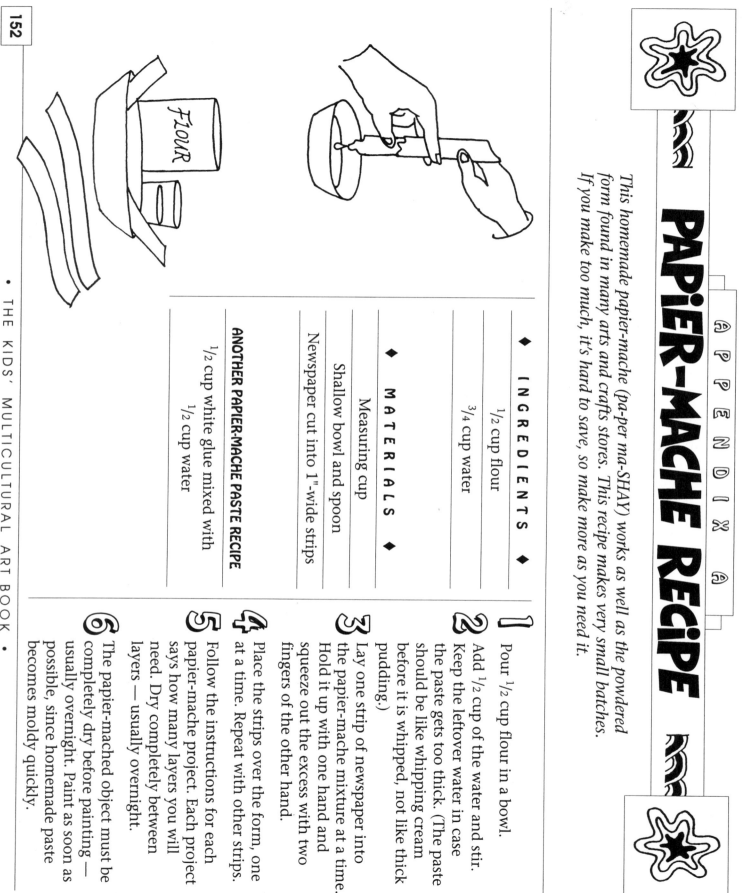

◆ INGREDIENTS ◆

¹/₂ cup flour

³/₄ cup water

◆ MATERIALS ◆

Newspaper cut into 1"-wide strips

Shallow bowl and spoon

Measuring cup

ANOTHER PAPIER-MACHE PASTE RECIPE

¹/₂ cup white glue mixed with
¹/₂ cup water

1 Pour ¹/₂ cup flour in a bowl.

2 Add ¹/₂ cup of the water and stir. Keep the leftover water in case the paste gets too thick. (The paste should be like whipping cream before it is whipped, not like thick pudding.)

3 Lay one strip of newspaper into the papier-mache mixture at a time. Hold it up with one hand and squeeze out the excess with two fingers of the other hand.

4 Place the strips over the form, one at a time. Repeat with other strips.

5 Follow the instructions for each papier-mache project. Each project says how many layers you will need. Dry completely between layers — usually overnight.

6 The papier-mached object must be completely dry before painting — usually overnight. Paint as soon as possible, since homemade paste becomes moldy quickly.

SALT DOUGH RECIPE

Using clay to make three-dimensional objects is a wonderful way to use your hands. This easy salt dough recipe is just what you need to make your "clay" projects come to life. Follow the instructions for baking carefully.

◆ INGREDIENTS ◆

3 cups flour
(any kind except self-rising)

1¼ cups warm tap water

1 cup salt

◆ MATERIALS ◆

Measuring cup, bowl, and spoon

Wooden board or piece of wax paper taped to the table

Rolling pin
(or the side of a smooth glass)

Plastic knife

Items to make designs: toothpicks, pencil points, plastic fork

1 Pour 1 cup of salt into a bowl.

2 Add 1¼ cups warm tap water to the salt, stirring until the salt dissolves.

3 Add 3 cups of flour to this mixture. Stir.

4 Mix and knead the dough by working it with your hands, shaping and reshaping, until it is smooth and firm. Form it into a ball.

5 Use the dough right away or store it in a covered container in the refrigerator for up to a week.

To bake:

1 Have an older helper preheat the oven to 250°F. NEVER USE AN OVEN BY YOURSELF.

2 Use a rolling pin or the side of a large glass to roll out the dough. Don't make it too thick or it won't bake all the way through. Cut into pieces, press in designs, and make holes in the dough. Place pieces on a cookie sheet.

3 Bake small projects about 45 minutes to 1 hour. Large projects will take about 2 hours. Have an older helper check the dough once in a while.

4 When golden, use a potholder to remove from oven. Let cool before painting.

BiBLiOGRAPHY

Berdan, Frances F. *The Aztecs*. New York: Chelsea House, 1989.

Berliner, Nancy Zeng. *Chinese Folk Art*. Boston: A New York Graphic Society Book, Little, Brown and Co., 1986.

Bossert, Helmuth T. *Folk Art of Asia, Africa, Australia and the Americas*. New York: Rizzoli, 1990.

Comins, Jeremy. *Getting Started in African Crafts*. New York: Bruce Publ., 1971.

Constable, George, ed. *Mexico*. Amsterdam: Time-Life Books, 1985.

Dockstader, Frederick J. *Indian Art in America: The Arts and Crafts of the North American Indian*. Connecticut: New York Graphic Society, 1966.

Ekiguchi, Kunio, and Ruth S. McCreery. *A Japanese Touch for the Seasons*. Tokyo: Kodansha Intl., 1987.

Gillon, Werner. *A Short History of African Art*. London: Penguin, 1984.

Glubok, Shirley. *The Art of the Woodland Indians*. New York: Macmillan, 1976.

Hamlyn, Paul. *African Art*. Middlesex: Hamlyn, 1968.

Harvey, Marian. *Crafts of Mexico*. New York: Macmillan, 1973.

Joseph, Joan. *Folk Toys Around the World and How to Make Them*. New York: Parents' Magazine Press, 1972.

Lost Empires, Living Tribes. Washington, D.C.: National Geographic Society, Publ., 1982.

Manley, Seon. *Adventures in Making: The Romance of Crafts Around the World*. New York: Vanguard Press, 1959.

Maxwell, James A., ed. *America's Fascinating Indian Heritage*. Pleasantville, New York: Reader's Digest Assoc., 1978.

Morris, Walter F. Jr., Abrams, Harry N. *Living Maya*. New York: Harry N. Abrams Publishers, Inc., 1987.

National Museum of African Art. *The Art of West African Kingdoms*. Washington, D.C.: Smithsonian Institution Press, 1987.

National Museum of African Art, Smithsonian, Washington, D.C.

McNair, Sylvia. *Enchantment of the World: Korea*. Chicago: Childrens Press, 1986.

McNair, Sylvia. *Enchantment of the World: Thailand*. Chicago: Childrens Press, 1987.

Panyella, August, ed. *Folk Art of the Americas*. New York: Harry N. Abrams Publishers, Inc. 1981.

Phillips, Robert S., ed. *Funk & Wagnalls New Encyclopedia*. Funk & Wagnalls, MCMLXXI.

Pueblo to People Catalog. Spring 1992.

Saint-Gilles, Amaury. *Mingei: Japan's Enduring Folk Arts*. San Francisco: Heian Intl., Inc., 1983.

Shalant, Phyllis, and Julian Messner. *Look What We've Brought You From Vietnam*. New York, 1988.

The Story of Africa & Her Flags to Color. Santa Barbara: Bellerophon Books, 1991.

Talyarkhan, Natasha, and Dale Gunthrop, ed. *India: The Land and Its People*. London: Macdonald Educational, 1975.

Tanner, Clara Lee. *Southwest Indian Craft Arts*. Tucson: University of Arizona Press, 1968.

Tunis, Edward, and Thomas Y. Crowell, Publ. *Indians*. New York, 1959.

Whiteford, Andrew Hunter. *North American Indian Arts*. New York: Golden Press, 1990.

Wolfson, Evelyn. *From Abenaki to Zuni: A Dictionary of Native American Tribes*. New York: Walker and Co., 1988.

Yoo, Yushin, Dr. *Korea the Beautiful: Treasures of the Hermit Kingdom*. Los Angeles and Louisville: Golden Pond Press, 1987.

MORE GOOD BOOKS FROM WILLIAMSON PUBLISHING

Kids Can!®

The following Kids Can!® books for ages 4 to 10 are each 160-178 pages, fully illustrated, trade paper, 11 x 8 ½, $12.95 US.

HAND-PRINT ANIMAL ART
by Carolyn Carreiro ($14.95)

CUT-PAPER PLAY!
Dazzling Creations from Construction Paper
by Sandi Henry

Early Childhood News Directors' Choice Award

VROOM! VROOM!
Making 'dozers, 'copters, trucks & more
by Judy Press

COOL CRAFTS & AWESOME ART!
A Kids' Treasure Trove of Fabulous Fun
by Roberta Gould

Oppenheim Toy Portfolio Best Book Award
American Bookseller Pick of the Lists
Benjamin Franklin Best Nonfiction Award

SUPER SCIENCE CONCOCTIONS
50 Mysterious Mixtures for Fabulous Fun
by Jill Frankel Hauser

THE KIDS' NATURE BOOK *(Newly Revised)*
365 Indoor/Outdoor Activities and Experiences
by Susan Milord

Benjamin Franklin Best Multicultural Book Award
Parents' Choice Approved
Skipping Stones Multicultural Honor Award

THE KIDS' MULTICULTURAL COOKBOOK
Food & Fun Around the World
by Deanna F. Cook

Parents' Choice Approved
Dr. Toy Best Vacation Product Award

KIDS GARDEN!
The Anytime, Anyplace Guide to Sowing & Growing Fun
by Avery Hart and Paul Mantell

Winner of the Oppenheim Toy Portfolio Best Book Award
American Bookseller Pick of the Lists

THE KIDS' SCIENCE BOOK
Creative Experiences for Hands-On Fun
by Robert Hirschfeld and Nancy White

Parents' Choice Gold Award
American Bookseller Pick of the Lists
Winner of the Oppenheim Toy Portfolio Best Book Award

THE KIDS' MULTICULTURAL ART BOOK
Art & Craft Experiences from Around the World
by Alexandra M. Terzian

KIDS' COMPUTER CREATIONS
Using Your Computer for Art & Craft Fun
by Carol Sabbeth

Dr. Toy Best Vacation Product
Parents' Choice Gold Award
Parents Magazine Parents' Pick

Little Hands®

The following *Little Hands*® books for ages 2 to 6 are each 144 pages, fully illustrated, trade paper, 10 x 8, $12.95 US.

MATH PLAY!
80 Ways to Count & Learn
by Diane McGowan and Mark Schrooten

American Bookseller Pick of the Lists

RAINY DAY PLAY!
Explore, Create, Discover, Pretend
by Nancy Fusco Castaldo

FUN WITH MY 5 SENSES
Activities to Build Learning Readiness
by Sarah A. Williamson

Children's BOMC Main Selection

THE LITTLE HANDS ART BOOK
Exploring Arts & Crafts with 2- to 6-Year-Olds
by Judy Press

Parents' Choice Approved
Early Childhood News Directors' Choice Award

SHAPES, SIZES, & MORE SURPRISES!
A Little Hands Early Learning Book
by Mary Tomczyk

Parents' Choice Approved

The Little Hands BIG FUN CRAFT Book
Creative Fun for 2- to 6-Year-Olds
by Judy Press

Parents' Choice Approved

THE LITTLE HANDS NATURE BOOK
Earth, Sky, Critters & More
by Nancy Fusco Castaldo

Parents' Choice Gold Award
Benjamin Franklin Best Juvenile Nonfiction Award

KIDS MAKE MUSIC!
Clapping and Tapping from Bach to Rock
by Avery Hart and Paul Mantell

American Bookseller Pick of the Lists

KIDS' CRAZY CONCOCTIONS
50 Mysterious Mixtures for Art & Craft Fun
by Jill Frankel Hauser

Winner of the Oppenheim Toy Portfolio Best Book Award
Skipping Stones Nature & Ecology Honor Award

EcoArt!
Earth-Friendly Art & Craft Experiences for 3- to 9-Year-Olds
by Laurie Carlson

KIDS COOK!
Fabulous Food for the Whole Family
by Sarah Williamson and Zachary Williamson

THE KIDS' WILDLIFE BOOK
Exploring Animal Worlds through Indoor/Outdoor Crafts & Experiences
by Warner Shedd

HANDS AROUND THE WORLD
365 Creative Ways to Build Cultural Awareness & Global Respect
by Susan Milord

KIDS CREATE!
Art & Craft Experiences for 3- to 9-Year-Olds
by Laurie Carlson

Parents Magazine Parents' Pick

KIDS LEARN AMERICA!
Bringing Geography to Life with People, Places, & History
by Patricia Gordon and Reed C. Snow

American Bookseller Pick of the Lists

ADVENTURES IN ART (Newly Revised)
Art & Craft Experiences for 8- to 13-Year-Olds
by Susan Milord

Baby

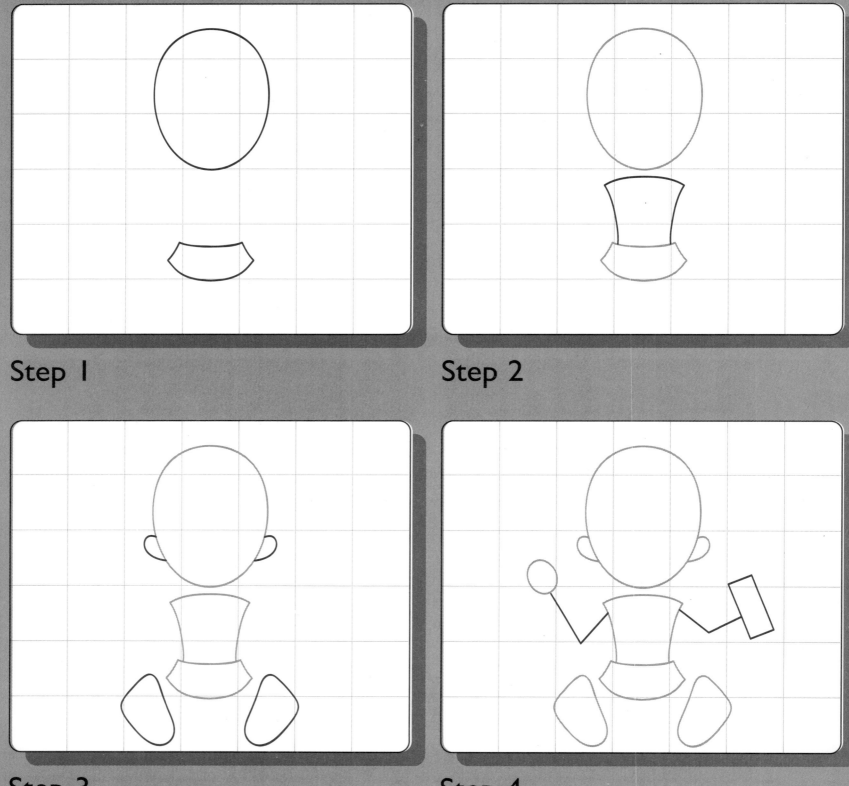

Step 1

Step 2

Step 3

Step 4

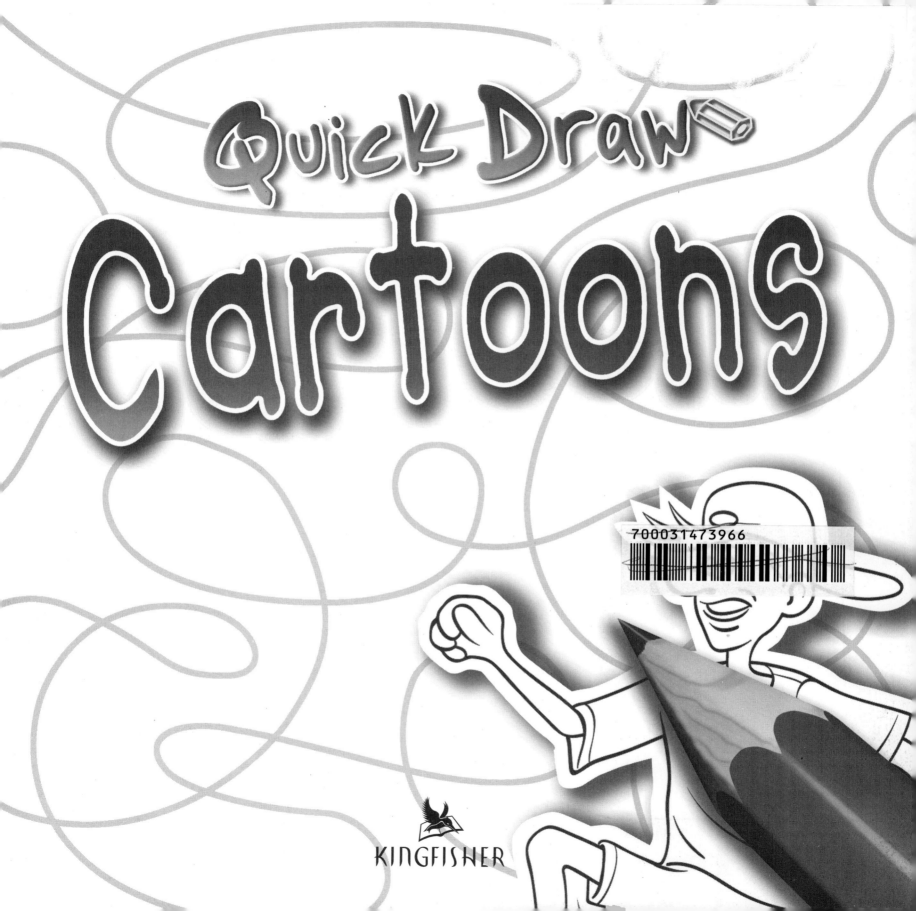

How to use this book

1. Trace the grid opposite. You can use any size of paper as long as the grid proportions are the same as the one in this book. The grid squares will help you position your drawing and ensure the different stages are correctly scaled.

2. Use a light pencil line to draw. That way you can rub out the lines much more easily.

3. Copy the shapes in step one, then add the new shapes in step two and so on. As you add each step, your picture will begin to take shape.

4. When you have copied each step, rub out the extra lines from the earlier step — to eventually reveal the final shape (as shown in the final step).

5. Now colour in your finished picture.

As you become more confident, you may find that you don't need the grid squares any more. You may wish to add your own finishing touches to the illustrations, such as background plants, to create a scene.

Step 5

Step 6

Step 7

Step 8

Cat

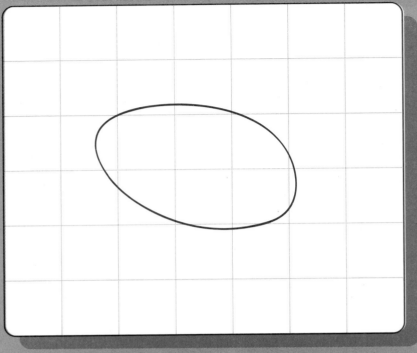

Step 1

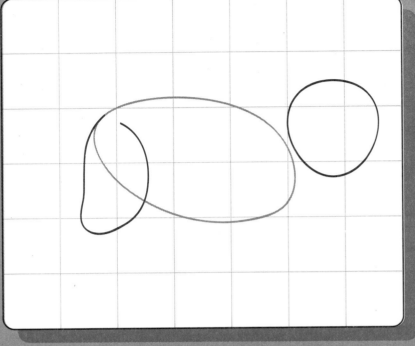

Step 2

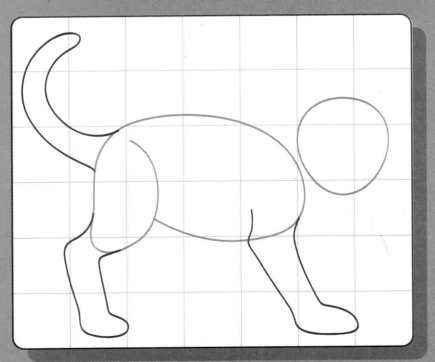

Step 3

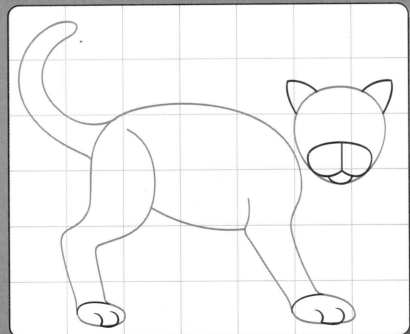

Step 4

Step 5

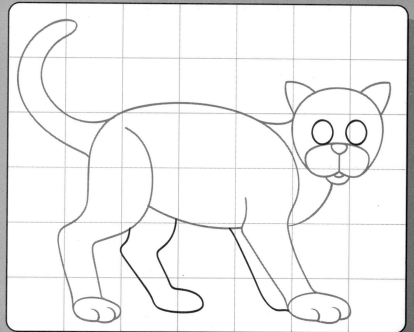

Step 6

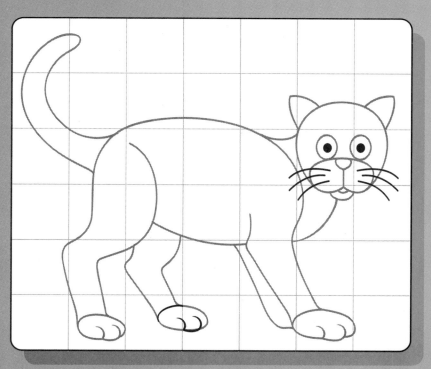

Step 7

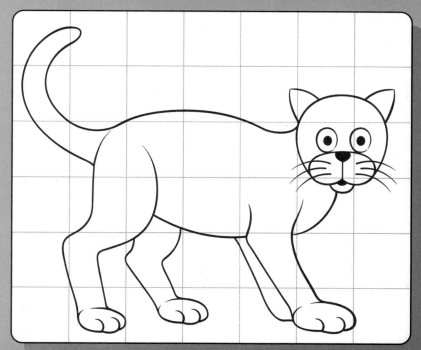

Step 8

Dog

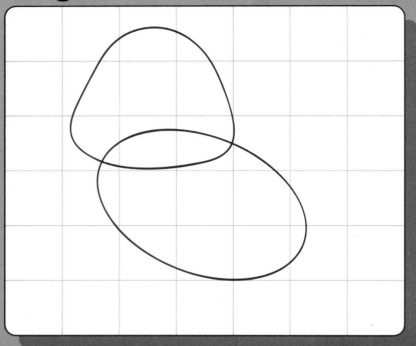

Step 1

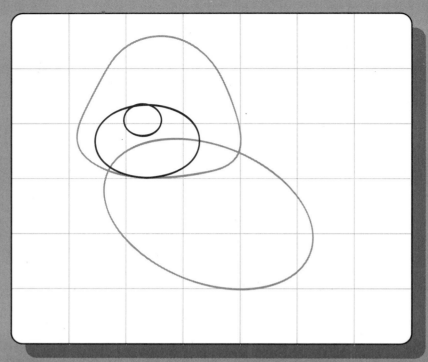

Step 2

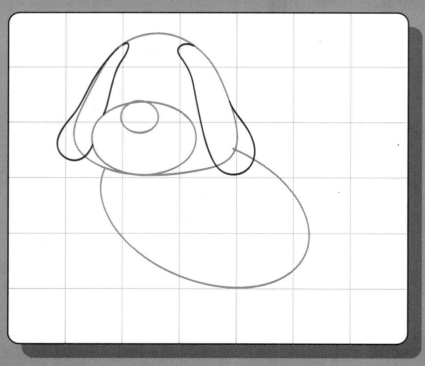

Step 3

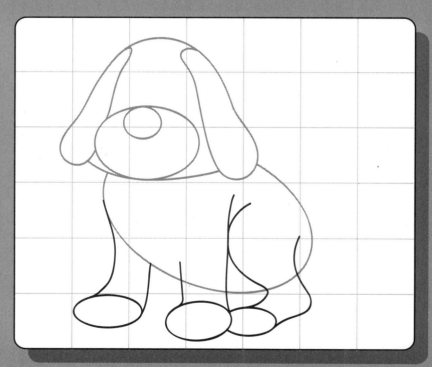

Step 4

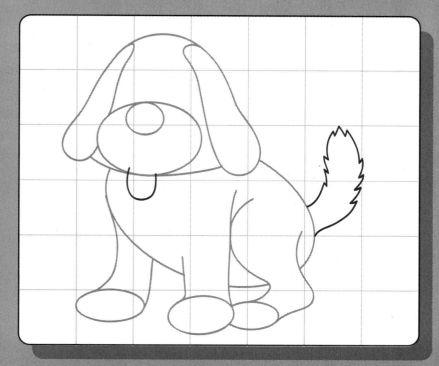

Step 5

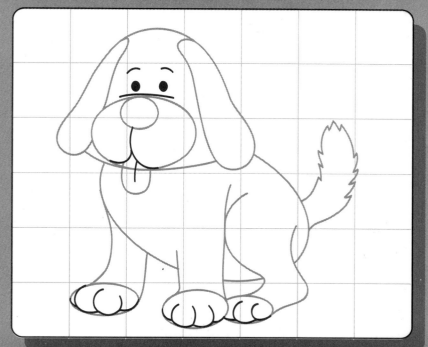

Step 6

Step 7

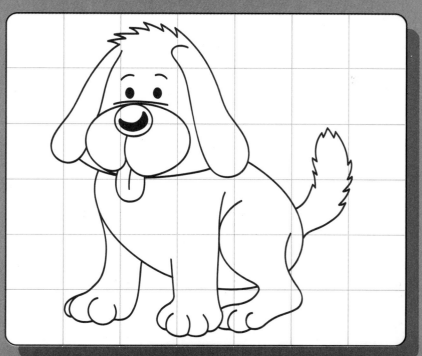

Step 8

Bear

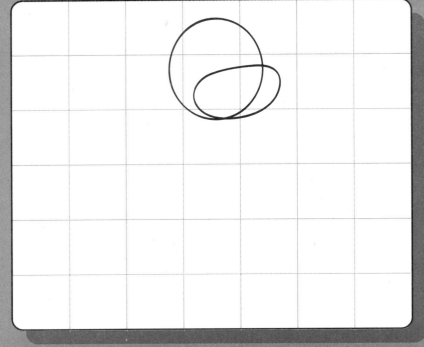

Step 1

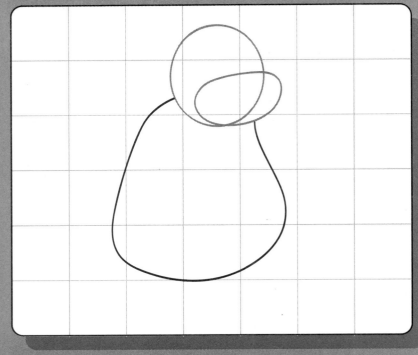

Step 2

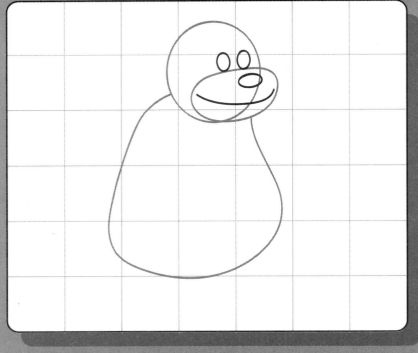

Step 3

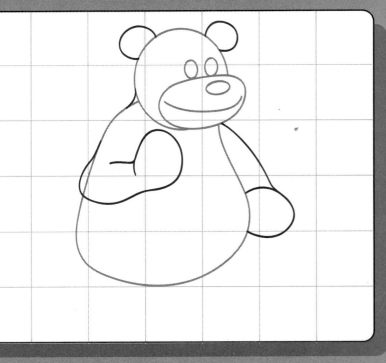

Step 4

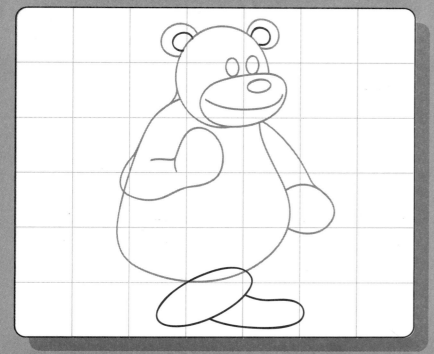

Step 5

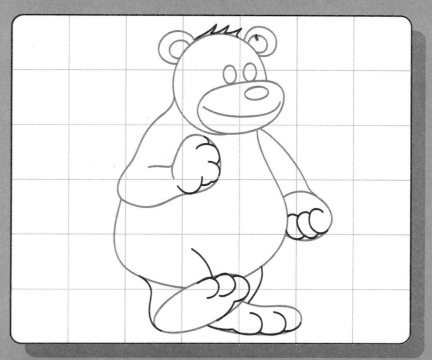

Step 6

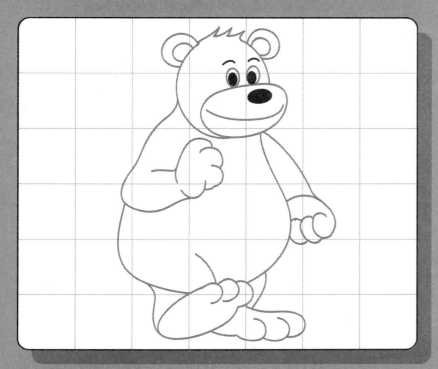

Step 7

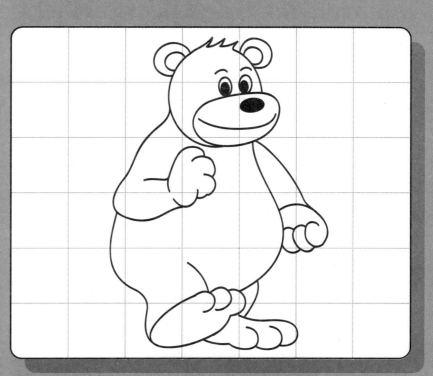

Step 8

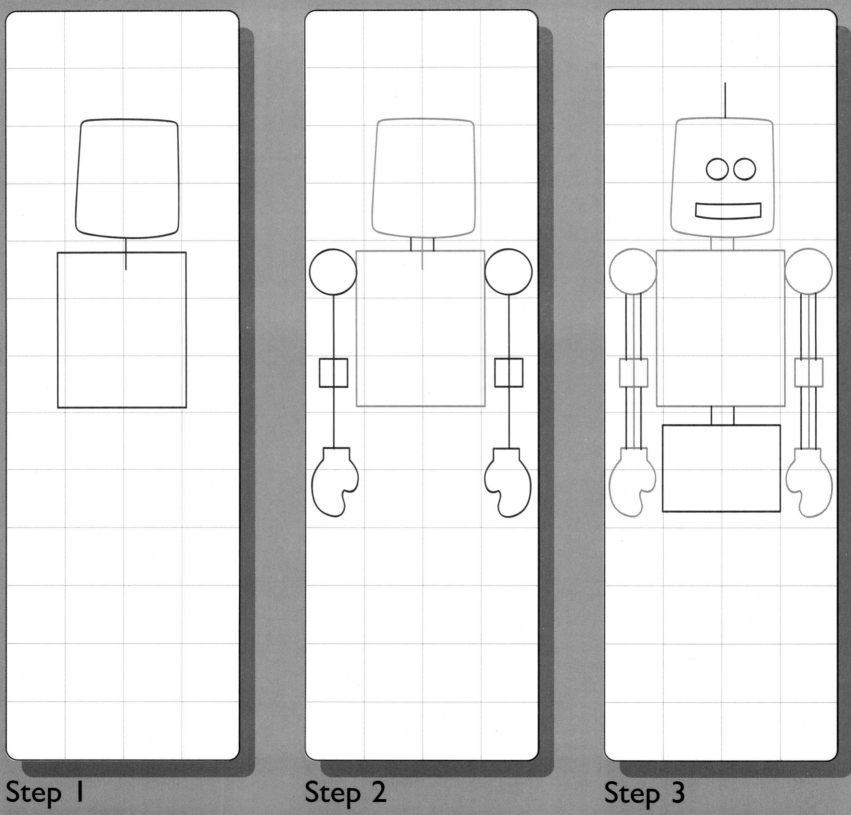

Step 1

Step 2

Step 3

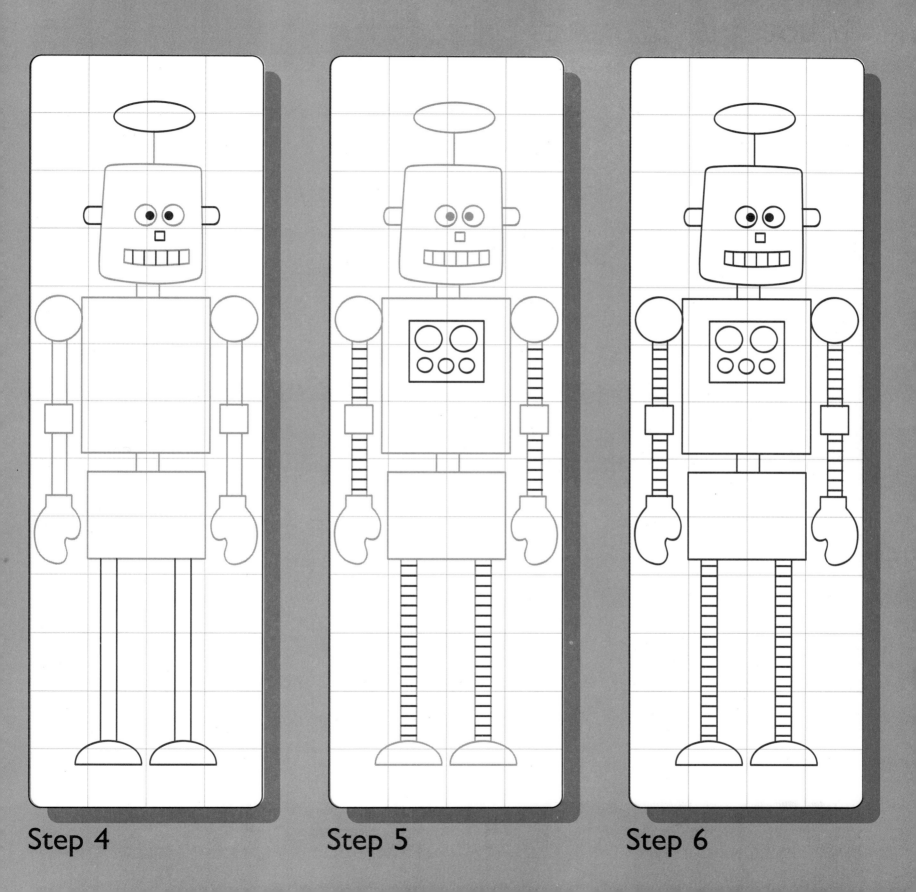

Step 4   Step 5   Step 6

Caveman

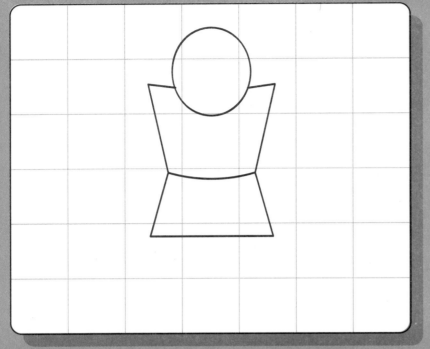

Step 1

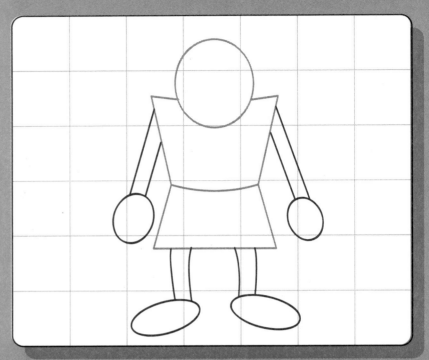

Step 2

Step 3

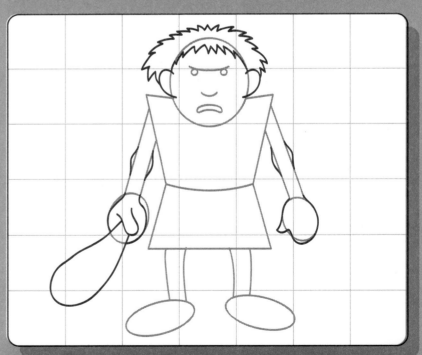

Step 4

Step 5

Step 6

Step 7

Step 8

Alien

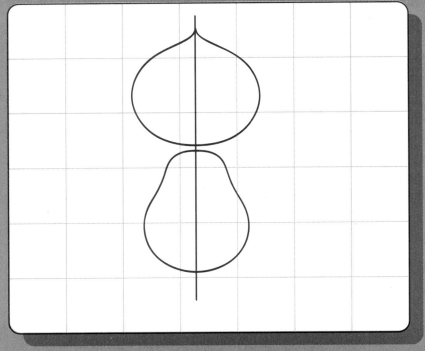

Step 1

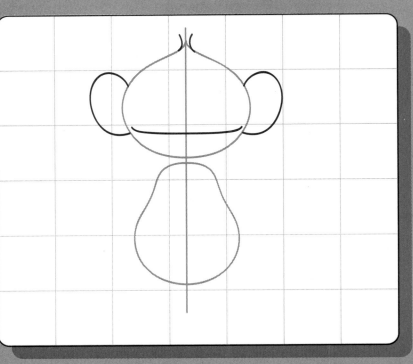

Step 2

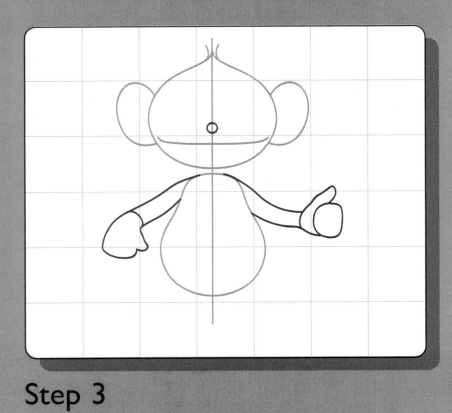

Step 3

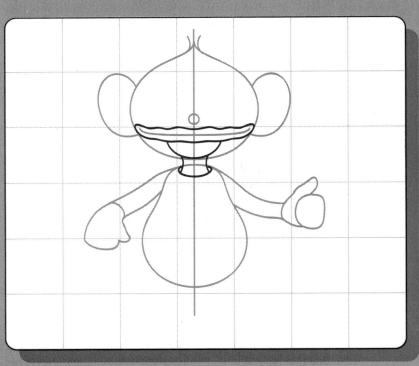

Step 4

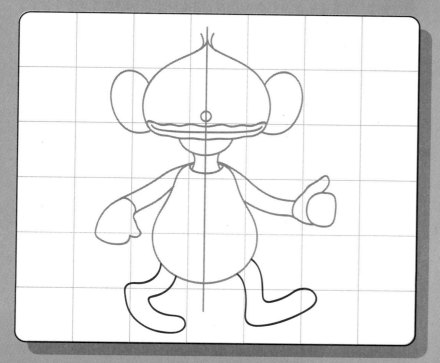

Step 5

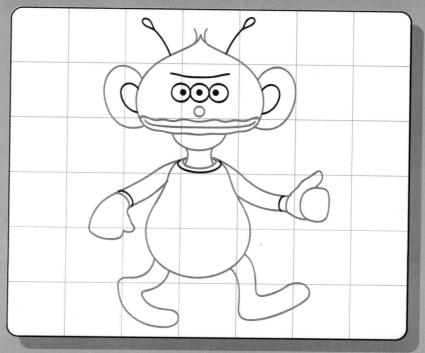

Step 6

Step 7

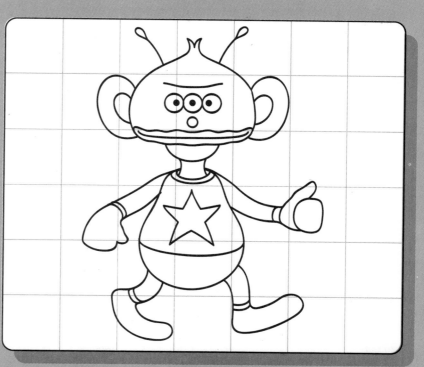

Step 8

Cyclist

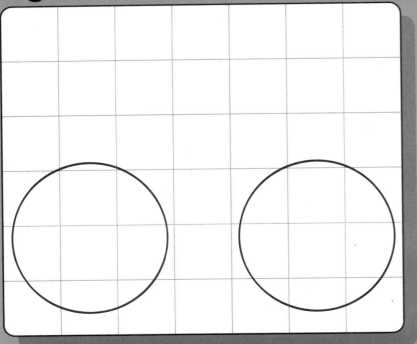

Step 1

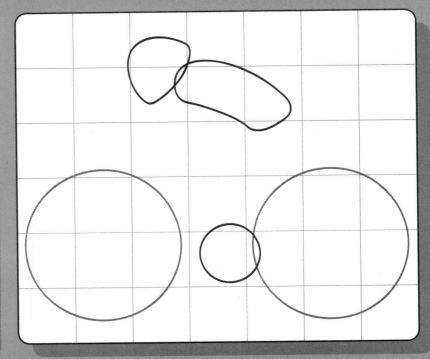

Step 2

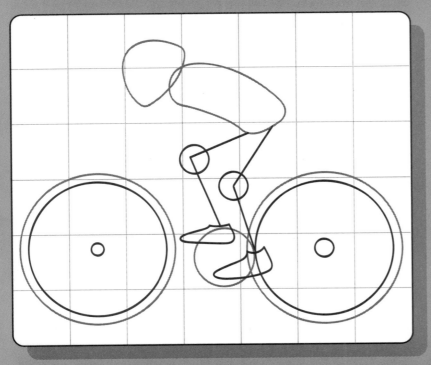

Step 3

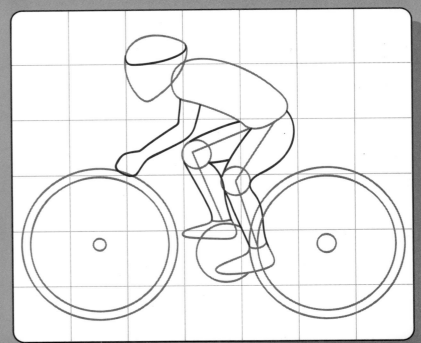

Step 4

Step 5

Step 6

Step 7

Step 8

Clown

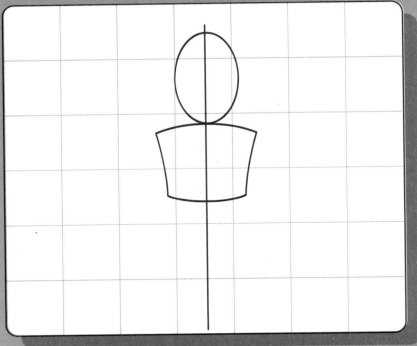

Step 1

Step 2

Step 3

Step 4

Step 5

Step 6

Step 7

Step 8

Skateboarder

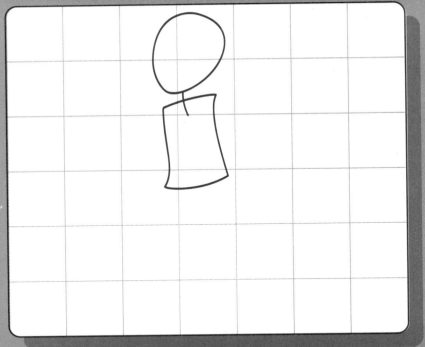

Step 1

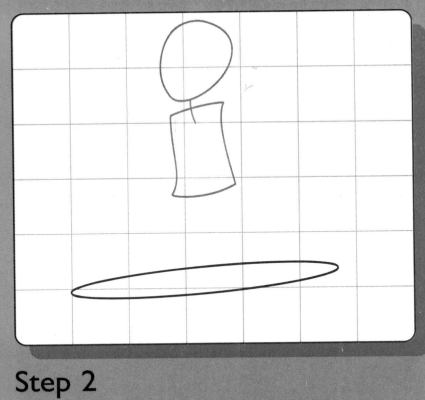

Step 2

Step 3

Step 4

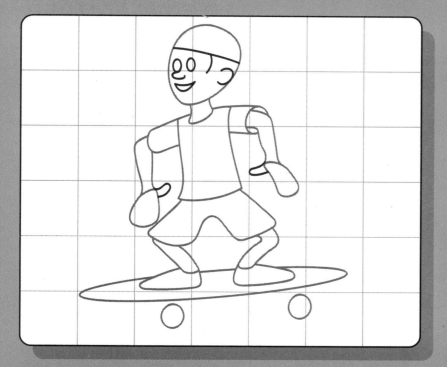

Step 5

Step 6

Step 7

Step 8

Monkey

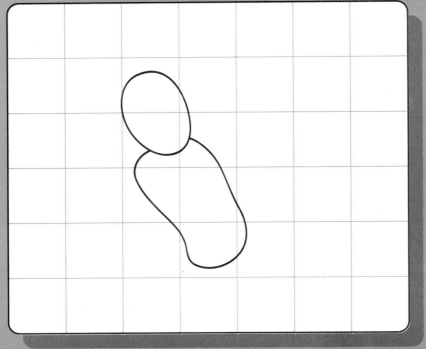

Step 1

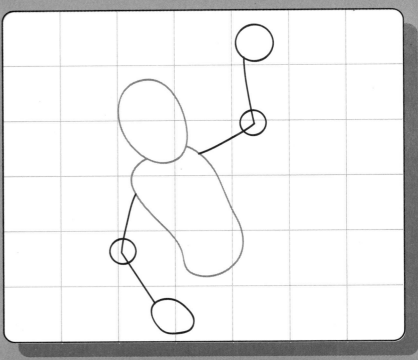

Step 2

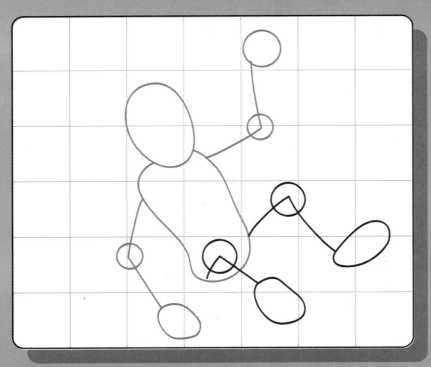

Step 3

Step 4

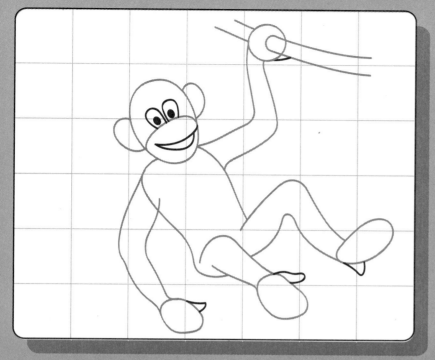

Step 5

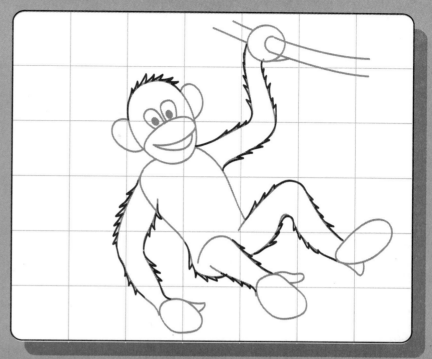

Step 6

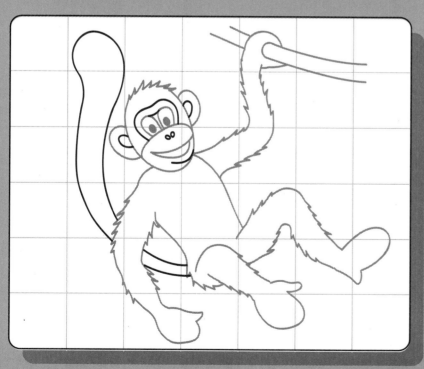

Step 7

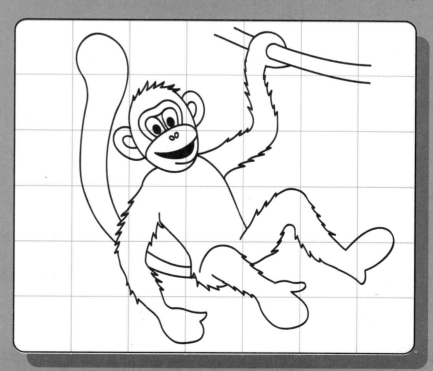

Step 8

Running boy

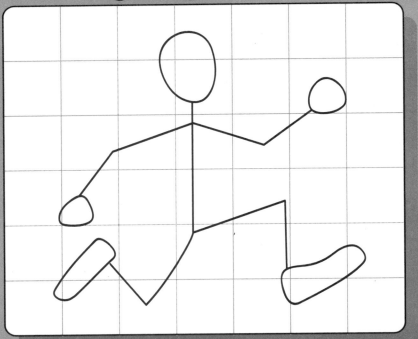

Step 1

Step 2

Step 3

Step 4

Step 5

Step 6

Step 7

Step 8

Astronaut

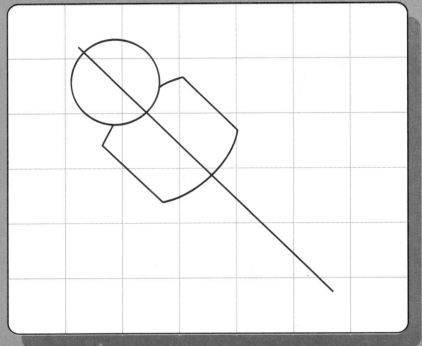

Step 1

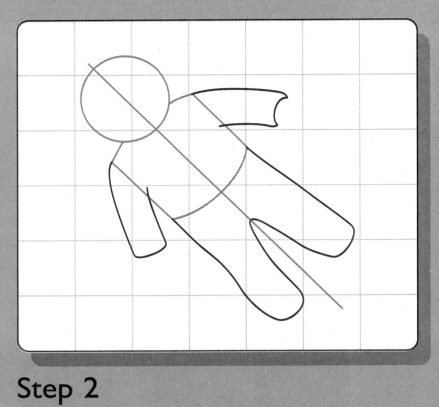

Step 2

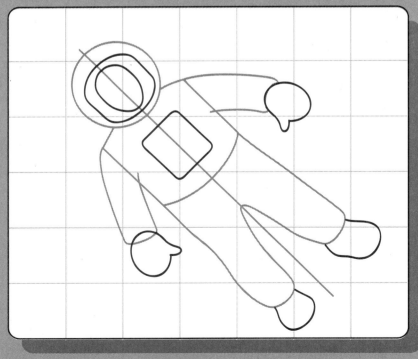

Step 3

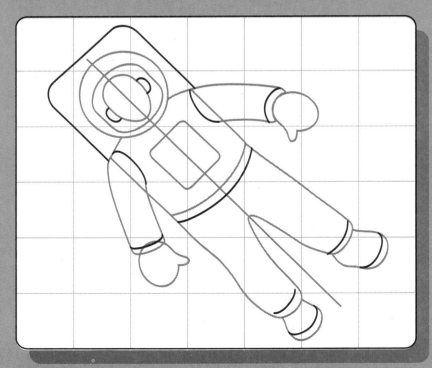

Step 4

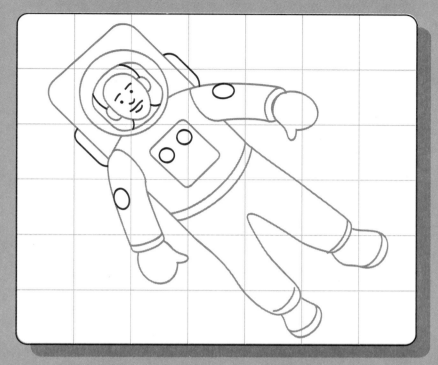

Step 5

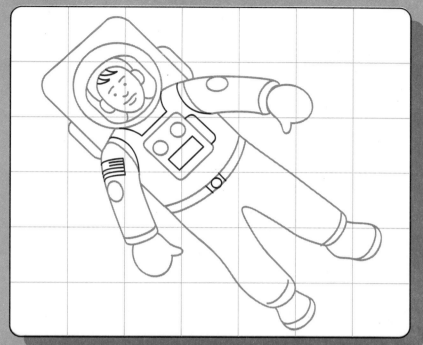

Step 6

Step 7

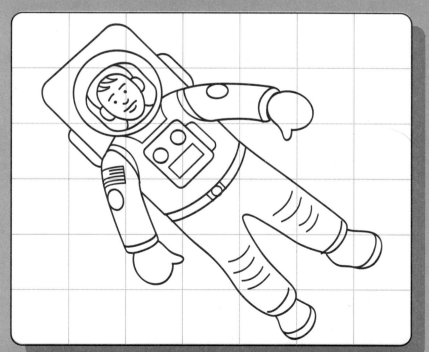

Step 8

Superhero

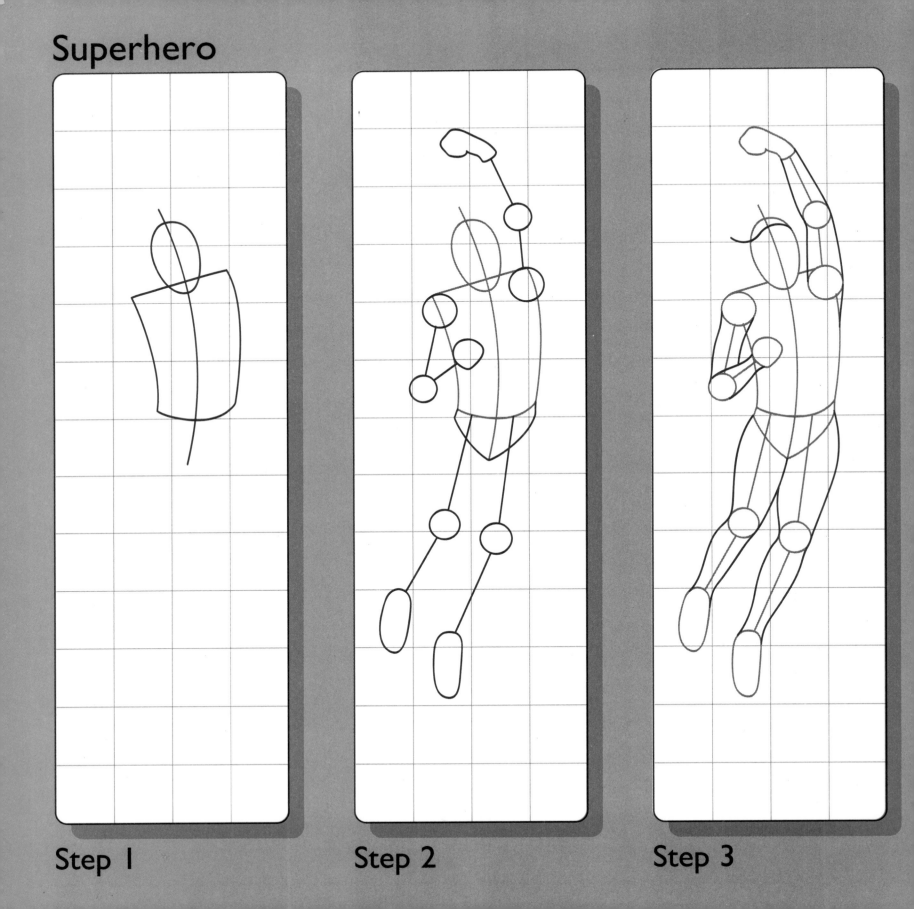

Step 1

Step 2

Step 3

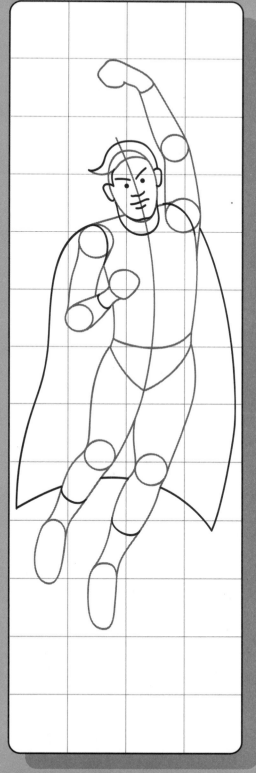

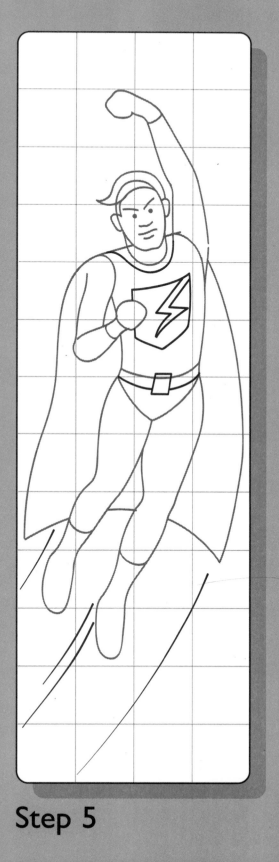

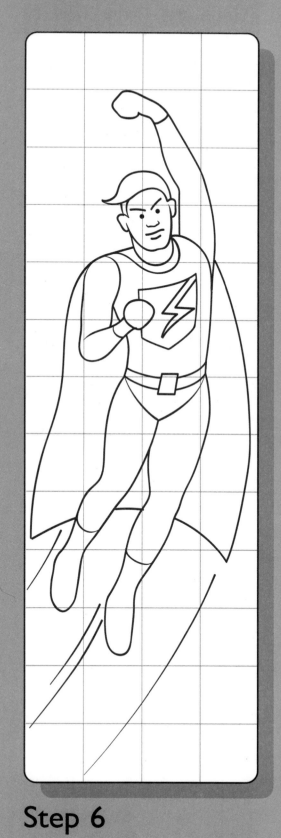

Step 4

Step 5

Step 6

KINGFISHER

Kingfisher Publications Plc
New Penderel House
283–288 High Holborn
London WCIV 7HZ
www.kingfisherpub.com

First published by Kingfisher Plc 2007
10 9 8 7 6 5 4 3 2 1

1TR/0907/THOM/IGS(SCHOY)/120BLT/C

Copyright © Kingfisher Publications Plc 2007

ISBN 978 0 7534 1607 5

Produced for Kingfisher by The Peter Bull Art Studio

For Kingfisher:
Associate Creative Director: Mike Davis
Designers: Ray Bryant and Emy Manby
Senior production controller: Jessamy Oldfield
DTP Manager: Nicky Studdart

A CIP catalogue record for this book is available from
the British Library.

Printed in India